It was a dark and stormy night ...

and I was working hard at my desk, when I was suddenly woken up by a strange ringing in my left ear. It was the telephone.

"Hello?" said the voice on the other end. "You've got to do something for me! I'm desperate!"

"Hi, Des!" I replied cheerily.
"No . . . no! My name isn't Des Perate!"
"Isn't it?"

It was outrageous! A man ringing me up with a false name? He was nothing but a telephoney!

"What is your name then?" I asked.

"Algernon Twistleton-Smythe."

"Then no wonder you're desperate."

"Listen. You must write a book for me about how to handle your dad."

"Must I?"

"Yes! Today!"

"But why should I write a book for you about how to handle my dad when you don't even know him?"

The phone went *Purrrrrr*. Either Algernon Twistleton-Smythe had put the receiver down, or he'd put his cat on the line to speak to me.

Then I remembered. Algernon Twistleton-Smythe was the name of my publisher and I had agreed to write a book for him by 1 January. Then I remembered something else. It was New Year's Eve tomorrow. I only had a day to write it!

There was a very good reason my publisher was desperate for me to write a book on how to handle your dad. His father had threatened to stop his pocket money for a month unless he did something about tidying up his bedroom.

Then I remembered another something else: the book was called. . .

Scholastic Children's Books,
Commonwealth House, 1-19 New Oxford Street,
London WC1A 1NU, UK

A division of Scholastic Ltd
London ~ New York ~ Toronto ~ Sydney ~ Auckland
Mexico City ~ New Delhi ~ Hong Kong

Published in this edition by Scholastic Ltd, 2002

First published in the UK by Scholastic Ltd, 1996
Text copyright © Roy Apps, 1996
Illustrations copyright © Nick Sharratt, 1996

ISBN 0 439 98230 8

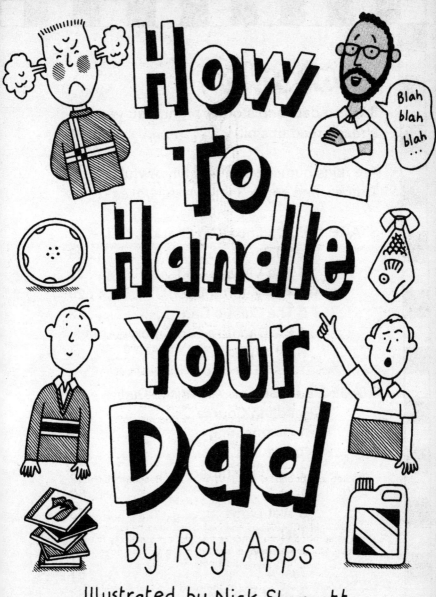

How To Handle Your Dad

Blah blah blah ...

By Roy Apps

Illustrated by Nick Sharratt

Hippo

Contents

Are dads human? Some Really Awful Truths – and Some Really Awful Jokes

You may find this difficult to believe, but there are actually some types of dad that are easy to handle. However, they're rather like a piece of half-cooked steak; that is they're very rare indeed. If you think you've got one of these types of dads, just cut out these two and a half pages and stick them some place where you can easily see them; like the end of your nose.

That way if someone asks you what type of dad you've got, you won't be stuck for an answer, you'll be stuck **to** an answer.

Then you can use the rest of this book to do some origami.

Or alternatively to do some 'orridgami.

Now where was I? Oh yes, at the top of page 8. But I'm not now, I'm half way down page 9. The four types of dad that are easy to handle are:

Type 1: The Christmas-type Father (aka Father Christmas)

Four fascinating facts about this dad-type
1 JOB: They go on lots of business trips to Lapland.
2 FAVE GEAR: Really crazy fur-lined red coats and hats all year round.

3 WHEELS: None. They use a sleigh.

4 FAVE FOOD: Anything, so long as it's not mince pies.

Typical Father Christmas conversation:
YOU: "What's that drifting out of the clouds onto our roof, Dad?"
FATHER CHRISTMAS: "Only rain dear! Ho! Ho! Ho!"

Type 2: The Godfather

Four fascinating facts about this dad-type
1 JOB: They work as violinists, or fiddlers at any rate.
2 FAVE GEAR: Black fur coats and shades. Crazy!

3 WHEELS: Black Mercedes
4 FAVE FOOD: Steak out

Typical Godfather conversation:
YOU: "Can I come for a ride in the car, Dad?"
GODFATHER: "Sure. Get in the boot."

Type 3: The Codfather

*Four fascinating facts
about this dad-type*
1 JOB: Something
Of-fish-all
2 FAVE GEAR:
Oil skins and
waders
3 WHEELS:
Turbot-powered
Jeep
4 FAVE FOOD: A
little fishy on a
little dishy.

Typical Codfather conversation:
CODFATHER: "What do you think of that, eh?"
YOU: "It's a bit small for bait isn't it, Dad?"
CODFATHER: "Bait! That's the fish I've just
caught!"

Type 4: The Crane Fly (aka Daddy-Long-Legs)

Four fascinating facts about this dad-type

1 JOB: Creeping out of the plug hole when you're having a bath.

2 FAVE GEAR: Trouser legs: preferably yours.

3 WHEELS: Eight legs

4 FAVE FOOD: Algae and double portion of french flies.

Typical daddy-long-legs conversation:
YOU: "Aaaaarghhhh!"

If your dad's a crane fly, it's incredibly easy to handle him. All you have to do is whisk on the tap.

Those of you whose dads are either Santa Clauses, Mafia bosses, fishermen or crane flies can stop reading now.

- - - cut here - - - - - - - - - - - - - - - - - -

Right. That's got rid of them. I hate those sort of people, don't you? "My daddy runs the Mafia, what does yours do?" They're so snobby!

If you've got a pretty ordinary type of dad, there's no need to worry. Fortunately, help is not very far away. In fact, it's about twenty centimetres away. In front of your eyes. In the pages of this book.

The first thing to establish is what your dad is, given that he's not a Santa Claus, a Mafia boss, a fisherman or a crane fly. Now you probably think he's a member of the human race, but nothing could be farther – or indeed father – from the truth! The only race your dad's ever likely to be part of is the egg-and-spoon race on school sports day. Have a go at the following questionnaire:

QUESTIONNAIRE

I didn't mean that sort of having a go, I meant having a go at answering the questions:

1 You're in the front room with your dad. He's watching a really corny old film on the telly. You're playing with Freddy, your pet frog. In a corner of the room are some bookshelves your dad put up five minutes before. Match the objects to the descriptions below them.

(a) Your dad's knees
(b) Your dad's bookshelves
(c) Freddy the Frog
(d The old film on the telly

(i) Really creaky
(ii) Really croaky
(iii) Really creaky
(iv) Really creaky

2 What is this a picture of?

(a) Your dad's new creaky bookshelves ten seconds after he's put them up?
(b) Your Guy Fawkes bonfire?
(c) Your garden shed after it's been struck by a meteorite?

3 What does your dad do after going out for a five-minute jog?

(a) Collapse on the floor?
(b) Collapse on the sofa?
(c) Collapse onto his new bookshelves?

4 What does your dad say when your mum asks him if he's going to help her with the weekly shopping?

(a) "Aargh! My back! It's killing me!"
(b) "Oooh! My leg! It's my hamstring, I think!"
(c) "I was just going to try and put those bookshelves up . . . er . . . again."

5 Does your dad:

(a) live in a swamp?
(b) have slimy green scales all down his back?
(c) have teeth the size of phone books?

The answer to **1** is (a)=(iv);b=(iii);(c)=(ii);d=(i).

If you have answered (a) to question **2** then your dad obviously isn't human, but he isn't an alien either. I mean what kind of self-respecting alien would make such a mess of putting up bookshelves?

If you answered (a), (b) or (c) to question **3** then again, your dad isn't a human. He's hardly a he-man either, is he?

If you answered (a), (b) or (c) to question **4** then, once again, your dad isn't a human being. Though he may be a hu-moan being.

And there you have it. Dads tend to be creaky, unable to go very far and not in a fit state to take your mum shopping. I warned you the truth about dads was really awful and the awful truth of the matter is, of course, that dads are OLD CROCKS! Unless you answered (a) (b) or (c) to question **5**, in which case your dad is not an old crock, but an OLD CROC.

old crock

old croc

In which case, you'd better not let him catch you reading this book, because he's likely to bite your head off. There. I warned you that the jokes were really awful too, didn't I?

So if you're going to have any chance at all of learning how to handle your dad, you've got to think of him not so much as a dear old pa, but more like a dear old car.

Now if you have trouble handling an old crock car, the solution is easy peasy. You take it along to the famous Scottish motor engineer A. McHannick.

To be able to help people sort out problems with their old crock dads though, is much more difficult. It requires a person of great skill, intelligence, fortitude, wit, charm and modesty. But that's enough about my fantastic qualities as a human being. Let me tell you about my work. I go about the place helping people with all sorts of problems they may have with their old crock dads. In other words, I'm a Mobile Old Crock Doc.

If you want to know everything there is to know about how to handle your dad, all you need to do is to follow E.I. DADDIO's Advanced Dad Handling Course. It comes in two easy stages – and four hard ones.

Of course, you do have to be particularly brilliant, intelligent and brainy to take the course, so just to make sure you're up to it, there is an advanced aptitude test to complete before you begin:

E.I. DADDIO'S ADVANCED DAD HANDLING COURSE APTITUDE TEST

Answer **all** questions
Time allowed: A couple of minutes – or if you need longer, a hundred and twenty one seconds.

1 Write your name in the space provided.

ANSWER . . . .
. . . .

2 Antidisestablishmentarianism is a very long word. How do you spell it?

ANSWER . . . .
. . . .

Now turn over for the right answers.

No, I didn't mean turn the book over. I meant turn the page over. . .

That's better.

The answers to the aptitude test are:

1 Your name in the space provided.
2 It.

How did you do?

Both answers right? Good. Go straight to page 21.
One answer right? Not bad. Go straight to the next page.
Both answers wrong? Pretty good. Now follow the arrows. . .

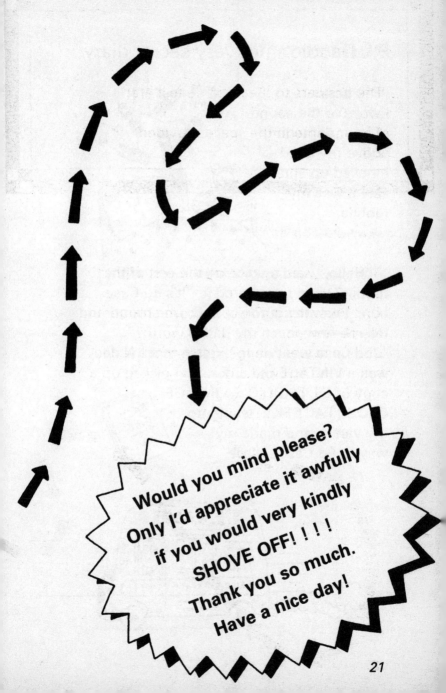

E.I. Daddio's not very secret diary

0830 hours
I woke to the sound of strange ringing above my head. I looked up and saw it was my mobile.

"Hello," said a voice on the end of the mobile when I answered it. "It's Ed Case here. I wonder if you could come round and tell me how much my dad is worth?"

Ed Case went on to explain that his dad was a VINTAGE old crock. So I picked up a copy of E.I. DADDIO'S VINTAGE CROCK FACT FILE, leapt into my van — and made my way to Ed Case's place.

How To Handle Your Dad : Stage One

E.I. DADDIO'S OLD CROCK FACT FILE:

Dad type 1: **The Vintage Dad**

An Old Ford Popular

A favourite vintage dad; known as: Old Ford Pop

Vintage crocks were built between 1940-50: that is, during or just after the war, when parts were scarce. So most of them were fitted with second-hand or used parts. That's why Ed's gran says things to his mum about his dad like:

GRAN: I always said he
had his Uncle Bert's ears.

Vintage crocks are aka: old bangers. They
are known as old bangers for two reasons.
The first reason is because their skin
resembles that of an ancient sausage i.e.
it's all wrinkly.

old sausage   old dad

The second reason vintage dads are known
as old bangers is that they are built from
fireworks and can explode at any time. This
is what happened when I was in the kitchen
with Ed. Suddenly his dad came in. Quickly,
I realized it was time to retire to a safe
distance behind the fridge to watch the
display. . .

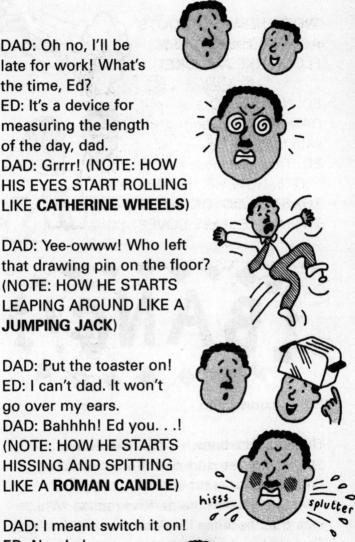

DAD: Oh no, I'll be late for work! What's the time, Ed?

ED: It's a device for measuring the length of the day, dad.

DAD: Grrrr! (NOTE: HOW HIS EYES START ROLLING LIKE **CATHERINE WHEELS**)

DAD: Yee-owww! Who left that drawing pin on the floor? (NOTE: HOW HE STARTS LEAPING AROUND LIKE A **JUMPING JACK**)

DAD: Put the toaster on!

ED: I can't dad. It won't go over my ears.

DAD: Bahhhh! Ed you. . .! (NOTE: HOW HE STARTS HISSING AND SPITTING LIKE A **ROMAN CANDLE**)

hisss

splutter

DAD: I meant switch it on!

ED: No, dad.

DAD: Then I will!

(NOTE: HOW HE SHOOTS
ACROSS THE KITCHEN
FLOOR LIKE A **ROCKET**)

ED: No, dad!
DAD: What's wrong
with the thing?
ED: There's a loose —
(NOTE: HOW HE THUMPS THE
TOASTER. NO, ON SECOND
THOUGHTS, TAKE COVER! ! !)

ED: — connection.

Oh dear, that blew it – the fuse that is.
"I'm still in the dark about how much my
dad is worth," said Ed.
"We're all still in the dark," I replied. Which
was true, because Ed's dad was still trying to
find his way to the fuse box.
    Once the lights were back on, I was able to
give Ed a copy of my valuation report.

E.I. DADDIO'S VALUATION REPORT ON HOW MUCH VINTAGE DADS ARE WORTH:

For fifty-one weeks of the year, absolutely zilch. But during the week of 5 November you can make stacks of dosh by hiring them out as One Man Firework Displays.

0900 hours
A regular customer of mine, Annie Oldiron called. "Can you come round and give my dad an annual check up?"
"Of course," I replied, "which of his annuals would you like me to check up; *The Wolf Cub Annual 1959, The Blue Peter Annual 1962* or *The Cracker Annual 1995*?" Then Annie explained that she wanted to make sure that her dad, who was a VETERAN old crock, wasn't falling to bits.

It was time to hit the road again. . .

I gave Annie Oldiron a few notes about her veteran dad:

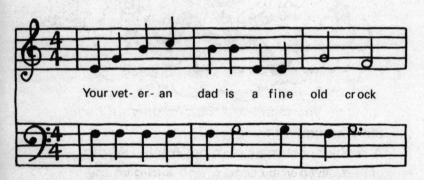

Your vet-er-an   dad is   a   fine   old   cr ock

Then after inspecting him, I gave her some more notes about her veteran dad.

E.I. DADDIO'S OLD CROCK FACT FILE:

Dad type 2: **The Veteran Dad**

A typical veteran dad, known as a La-Da

A posh version of the La-da, known as the La-Di-Da

Veteran crocks were built between 1950 and 1960. Just as some veteran cars were built so you could feel the sun on your head, so were veteran dads.

Nothing on top

Nothing on top

Note the shining chrome

Note the shining dome*

As you can see, Annie Oldiron's dad does have some hair on top, though. But I've instructed her to check it every day. After all, there's a great deal of truth in the old saying, "Hair today, gone tomorrow."

Veteran crock cars have terrible old chokes which make them groan:

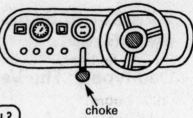

choke

How do you make a Swiss Roll?

Push him down a mountain!

joke

Veteran crock dads have terrible old jokes which make *you* groan.

Another quaint feature of veteran crocks is their indicator arms.

left

right

Just tidy that up!

Off you go, you'll be late for school!

Upstairs to your bedroom!

He's your gerbil, get down there and find him!

There was no doubt about it. Annie Oldiron's veteran dad certainly had a point. In fact, he had about four of them!

1000 hours
It was time to head for the station where I had planned to catch up with Noah Wunsin's classic dad. The reason Noah's dad was at the station was that he was the third type of dad – that is a CLASSIC dad.* However, whereas other classic dads try to keep in condition by weight training, Noah's dad tries to keep in condition by train waiting.

Weight training   Train waiting

Here are a few very useful facts and quite a lot more not very useful facts on this type of old pa.

*I hope you're taking all this in, 'cos I shall be asking questions later. On page 34 to be precise.

E.I. DADDIO'S OLD CROCK FACT FILE:

Dad type 3: **The Classic Dad**

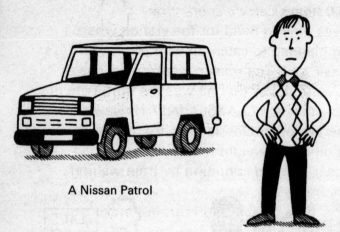

A Nissan Patrol

A familiar Classic dad;
known as a Nissan Papa-trol

Classic crocks were built between 1960 and 1970. They are known for their classic lines.

Note the classic lines

Note the lines

All classic crocks are G.T.S. types: that is, **G**one **T**o **S**eed. Although, like Noah's dad they can sometimes look a bit deflated, this isn't really a problem because they always carry a spare tyre:

spare tyre

spare tyre

classic car

classic pa

1100 hours
It was time for my mid-morning brake. . .

SCREECH!

Sorry that should've read "time for my mid-morning *break*". I munched away on some of my favourite dad-type snack – *pop* corn.

It is also time for you to try your hand at E.I. DADDIO's famous old Crock Spot Check or alternatively, you can try your brain at it:

E.I. DADDIO'S OLD CROCK SPOT CHECK:

Is your dad vintage, veteran or classic? It's easy to find out. Just give him E.I. DADDIO's famous OLD CROCK DOC spot check:

What does your dad put on his head in the morning?

(a) Tomato Ketchup   YES/NO
(b) A bowler hat   YES/NO
(c) Polish   YES/NO
(d) Millet   YES/NO
(e) Toothpaste   YES/NO

E.I. DADDIO's analysis of what the answers mean:

(a) If you've answered YES, your dad's an old banger. In other words, a vintage dad.
(b) If you've answered YES, your dad's not an old banger, but more likely an old banker.
(c) If you've answered YES, you've got a veteran dad with a chrome dome.
(d) If you've answered YES, your dad's Gone To Seed: he's a classic.
(e) If you've answered YES, your dad was still asleep when he went to the bathroom.

How To Handle Your Dad : Stage Two

E.I. DADDIO'S ADVANCED DAD HANDLING COURSE:

Dads are like an Agony Aunt's magazine column; they're full of problems. Problems for you, that is. E.I. DADDIO's advanced dad handling course will now take you through the tell-tale signs, causes and solutions to some of the most common problems, as recorded in E.I. DADDIO's Not Very Secret Diary of an Old Crock Doc.

E.I. Daddio's not very secret diary

1230 hours

Jim Nasticks called me out to say he was having trouble with his dad. "I'll be round in two shakes of a lamb's tail!" I said.

Unfortunately it took me twenty minutes to find a lamb and then another twenty minutes to catch it so that I could shake it's tail.

When I eventually arrived at Jim Nasticks' place, his dad's face spoke volumes:

"Is he about to blow a gasket?" asked Jim.

"You're getting warm," I replied. "Mind you, your dad's getting more than warm."

Yes, Jim's dad was displaying classic symptoms of overheating.

DAD PROBLEM 1: **OVERHEATING**

LOOK FOR THESE TELL-TALE SIGNS:
1 Your dad getting very hot under the collar.
2 Your dad getting very hot under his bonnet (if he wears one).

LISTEN OUT FOR THESE TELL-TALE NOISES:
"Grrrr!" "Yahhh!!!" "Borrr!!!"

WHAT CAUSES THE PROBLEM:
The slightest thing can cause a dad to overheat. For example, read what happened when I visited Ed Case's dad.* Another common cause is too much in the boot.

Who put these bricks in my boot?

*See pages 24-26.

"I've not put any bricks in my dad's boots," said Jim. "So what can be causing him to overheat like this?"

We went out to the garden to have another look at Mr Nasticks. As soon as I saw him, the cause of the overheating became pretty obvious – or rather not-very-pretty obvious.

"There's no doubt about it, Jim," I said. "Your dad's labouring in the wrong gear!"

Of course, just as with old cars, overheating results in old pas fuming.

old car   old pa

To help Jim Nasticks
with his overheating
dad, I sent him
this guide:

But she turned out to be as much use as a
chocolate tea pot, so I sent him this guide
instead:

E.I. DADDIO'S EASY STEP-BY-STEP GUIDE TO STOPPING DADS FROM OVERHEATING:

1 Check seriousness of overheating
problems. Is there:

(i) Steam coming ⟶ **YES** Serious over-
out of his ears? heating problem
NO
↓
(ii) Steam coming ⟶ **YES** Tell him to
out of his mouth? keep off the
NO Bombay Mix.
↓
(iii) Steam coming ⟶ **YES** He's put his jeans
out of his trouser leg? on while your mum was
still ironing them.

2 Cool him down, trying each of the following methods in turn:

(i) Say: "Father dear, your tea is cold. Would you like me to make you another cup?"

↓

Has he cooled down? → **NO**

↓

(ii) Say: "Father dear, I'd simply love to sit and listen with you to your wonderful 1965/1975/1995* Beatles album."

↓

Has he cooled down? → **NO**

↓

(iii) Turn the heating off when he's in the shower.

↓

Has he cooled down? → **NO**

↓

Sorry. There's nothing more you can do. Some vintage dads are just never going to get cool!

YES Success! Now all you've got to do is to find a potter's wheel, a kiln, two kilos of clay and you'll be able to make your dad another cup in no time at all! Well, about two days at any rate.

YES Success! Now all you've got to do is to find your double-thickness, industrial ear muffs.

YES Success! Now lock yourself in your bedroom for about four weeks.

*Delete as necessary, depending on whether you have a vintage, veteran or classic dad.

USEFUL TOOL FOR DEALING WITH OVERHEATING DADS:

A HOSE-PIPE: Particularly useful for trying to cool your dad down, if you haven't got a shower. Also, it means you can earn yourself some extra pocket money as a decorator. All you need to do is to shove the hose-pipe in your dad's ear while he's got a full head of steam, so to speak, and use your hose-pipe as a wallpaper stripper.

Before moving on to the next entry from my Not Very Secret Diary of an Old Crock Doc, complete the following test on OVERHEATING:

E.I. DADDIO'S ADVANCED DAD HANDLING COURSE: **TEST 1**

QUESTION: Which of the following things causes a dad to overheat?

TICK BOX

(a) wearing a woolly vest
in the middle of June

(b) wearing a woolly vest
in the middle of Woolworth's

(c) labouring in the wrong gear

(d) too much in the boot

ANSWERS:

(a) No points, but 10 pints. Of lemonade, that is, for your dad to help him cool down.

(b) This is more likely to cause you to overheat – with embarrassment.

(c) 1 point

(d) Another point

ENTER YOUR NUMBER OF
POINTS HERE IN THIS BOX:

E.I. Daddio's not very secret diary

1300 hours
The phone rang. My publisher, Algernon
Twistleton-Smythe was on the line.

"Get down Mr Twistleton-Smythe!" I
called to him out of the window.

"I want to end it all now!" he sobbed.

"Surely Mr Twistleton-Smythe, it's not that
bad!" I replied.

"Oh, yes it is," he said, "Particularly that
joke on page 42 about labouring in the
wrong gear."

"That was no joke," I said. "At least, it
wasn't for Jim Nasticks."

"Will you promise that the rest of your
book will be serious – in particular, no more
puns?"

"OK," I agreed, "no more puns, just bitta
pread, puttered scones and parmcakes."

Next to ring up was another regular customer of mine, Jilly Concarny. "It's my dad," she said, "I can't get him to budge at all."

When I got to Jilly Concarny's house, she took me into the sitting room to see her dad. But I couldn't. See him, that is. Then I noticed he was hiding behind the newspaper.

"Is it an expensive problem?" asked Jilly.

"Oh dear," I said.

"Is it?" said Jilly. "Well, I haven't got a lot of money."

"Don't worry," I told her. "I'll soon get your dad started."

DAD PROBLEM 2:
GETTING STARTED

LOOK OUT FOR THESE TELL-TALE SIGNS:
Your dad won't budge. Your appeals for a
new bike/horse/game of football/month's
holiday in Disneyland/help with
your maths homework etc seem
to leave him completely *unmoved*!

LISTEN OUT FOR THESE TELL-TALE NOISES:
"No!" "Never!" "Over my dead body!"

WHAT CAUSES THE PROBLEM:
Like old cars, old dads have to be started
with what's known as a *crank* handle. This is
hardly surprising as dads tend to have some
cranky ideas. For example:

YOU SAY: "Why have you
turned the telly off, Dad?"
YOUR DAD SAYS:
"Your homework is more
important than Neighbours!"
YOU THINK: *Cranky idea!*

YOU SAY: "But Dad everyone else is allowed
to put up Blur posters on their bedroom
wall."

Aw strewth Noelene!

YOUR DAD SAYS: "Yes, but not on the outside!"
YOU THINK: *What's his problem?*

YOU SAY (AS YOU COME IN FROM SCHOOL): "Hi, dad"
YOUR DAD SAYS: "Hello, sweetheart! Had a really exciting day at school?"
YOU THINK: *His mind's going.*

Now cranking an old car is a doodle:

Not to say a *doddle*, compared with trying to start an old dad. You see, in some ways, old dads are more like old clocks than old crocks. That is, you have to *wind them up.*

SOLUTION: E.I. DADDIO'S MOST COMMONLY USED DAD WIND-UPS:

YOU: "Dad! Gran's on the phone. She wants to come and stay for a month."
DAD (WOUND UP NICELY NOW): "Aargh! Tell her we're emigrating to the Outer Polly-Wollydoodle Islands!"

YOU: "But I've got my maths homework to do!"
RESULT: Your dad starts doing your maths homework. . .

AT LEAST UNTIL!!!!!
. . .He remembers that your gran's already staying with you.

YOU: "Dad! The bloke next door is just about to use a chain saw on your prize monkey puzzle tree."

DAD (WOUND UP NICELY NOW): "Right! Here I come. . .!" (DASHES OUT THE BACK)

YOU (ONCE OUTSIDE): "Oh! He seems to have gone. Here! You can play football/mend my bike etc now you're out here!"

RESULT: Your dad plays football/mends your bike etc. . .

AT LEAST UNTIL!!!!!

. . .He remembers that he hasn't got a prize monkey puzzle tree – only a prize monkey i.e. your big brother.

YOU: "Dad! Man United have got a new away strip."

DAD (WOUND UP NICELY NOW): "That's the fifteenth this season!"
YOU: "All my mates have got the strip."
(SOB. SOB. JUST LIKE PAUL GASCOIGNE)
RESULT: Your dad gives you some extra pocket money. . .

AT LEAST UNTIL!!!!!
. . .He remembers that you're an Arsenal supporter.

USEFUL SPARES TO HAVE IF YOUR DAD TENDS TO SUFFER FROM STARTING PROBLEMS:

A SPARE YES-U-CAN:
Particularly useful when your dad keeps saying "No-You-Can't". Just unlock his fuel cap (if he wears one) and fill up.

E.I. DADDIO'S ADVANCED DAD HANDLING COURSE: **TEST 2**

QUESTION: A handle for starting an old car and a vintage pa can both be described by the same word. Is the word:

TICK BOX

(i) crank ☐
(ii) knarc ☐
(iii) banger ☐

ANSWER:
(i) 1 point
(ii) No points. A knarc is a handle for making a car go backwards.
(iii) No points. Have you ever tried starting an old car with a sausage?

ENTER YOUR NUMBER OF
POINTS HERE IN THIS BOX: ☐

E.I. Daddio's not very secret diary

1430 hours
The phone rang. It was
my publisher Algernon
Twistleton-Smythe. Again.

"Do you know what the
time is?" he asked.

"Two thirty," I replied.

"Does it?" he answered. "You'd best get
yourself to the dentist then."

No sooner had I put
the phone down than
I heard someone
hammering on
the front door.

I went out and spoke to him. "Kindly put
that hammer away," I said.

"All right," said the boy who was standing
there, "but only if you come round and take
a look at my dad. I'm having such dreadful
problems with him."

"Jump into the van," I said.
The boy shook my hand.
"Noel Plates," he said.

"That's because I've passed my test,"
I replied somewhat huffily.

"No," said the boy, "that's my name. Noel
Plates."

When we got to Noel Plates' house, I
could hear his dad, even before we got in
the front door. In the kitchen, the situation
was like a writer of fairy stories; in other
words, grim. Noel's dad was holding a
bunch of flowers and singing a really soppy
song called "Bridge Over Troubled Water" to
Noel's mum.

"The problem with your dad," I whispered
to Noel, "is that he's rather like the troubled
water he's singing about. He's wet. Yes, your
dad is suffering — "

"And he's not the only one," butted in Noel.

—"from wet plugs," I said.

DAD PROBLEM 3: **WET PLUGS**

LOOK OUT FOR THIS TELL-TALE SIGN:
Your dad's eyes start to look all moony.

LISTEN OUT FOR THESE TELL-TALE NOISES:
Kissy-kissy. Slurp-slurp. Your dad starts to
make these really wet sounds just when
you've got your best friend round for tea. It's
so embarrassing!

WHAT CAUSES THE PROBLEM:
Not so much what, as who, because very
often the cause of the problem is your mum.
If your dad has a tendency to get wet plugs,
it's very obvious: you can hear it. One of the
most common times your dad will get wet
plugs is on a Friday night. He'll come home
from work with a bunch of flowers for your
mum and you'll hear:

YOUR DAD
(TO YOUR MUM):
"Hi, my sweetheart,
my pettikins!
I'm home."
(KISS. KISS. SLURP. SLURP.)
Mmmm. . .!
YOU THINK: *He sounds dreadful! So wet!*

Your mum cooking him his favourite dinner also causes wet plugs.

YOUR DAD (TO YOUR MUM): "Oh, my loveykins! Mmmm. . . My favourite! Lentil and Spinach Salad!"

YOU THINK: *He sounds dreadful! So wet!**

E.I. DADDIO'S REMEDIES FOR A DAD WITH WET PLUGS

QUICK REMEDY:
DRY HIS WET PLUGS:
By turning his hair dryer on him.
DISADVANTAGE OF
THIS REMEDY: Your
dad probably hasn't
got any hair let alone
a hair dryer.

*But not as dreadful nor as wet as the Lentil and Spinach Salad.

ALTERNATIVE REMEDY:
JUMP START
YOUR DAD (TO YOUR MUM): "Oh, my loveykins! Mmmm. . . My favourite! Lentil and Spinach Salad."
YOU THINK: *He sounds dreadful! So wet!*

NOW! ! ! You start jumping up and down.
YOUR DAD (HORRIFIED):
"What's wrong with her/him?"
YOU: "It's all this rabbit food you keep giving me. I think I'm turning into a jive bunny!"

RESULT: Your dad stops calling your mum soppy things like pettikins etc and starts calling you stroppy things like nit wit, bird brain etc.

E.I. DADDIO'S ADVANCED DAD HANDLING COURSE: **TEST 3**

QUESTION: Which of the following noises indicate that your dad's got wet plugs?

TICK BOX

(a) pettikins! ☐
(b) pottikins! ☐
(c) slurp ☐
(d) burp ☐
(e) sweetheart ☐
(f) sweat heart ☐

ANSWERS:

(a) 1 point

(b) No points. This is what you call your dad after he's tried explaining one of his cranky ideas.

(c) 1 point

(d) No points. Your dad's been at that Lentil and Spinach Salad again.

(e) 1 point

(f) No points. This is what your mum probably calls your dad if he's been wearing a woolly vest in June. (See Test 1)

ENTER YOUR NUMBER OF
POINTS HERE IN THIS BOX: ☐

E.I. Daddio's not very secret diary

1500 hours
The phone rang again.

"Hello," said the voice at the other end, "it's Jilly again."

"Yes, it is," I replied. "But then it is the middle of winter."

"No, it's Jilly Concarny, I rang earlier."

"So you did."

"And now I'm ringing you again."

"So you are. Are you still having problems getting your dad started?"

"No, just the opposite. I'm having problems stopping him. He just keeps going on and on."

"Sounds like his battery," I said.

"Please hurry," said Jilly.

"Don't worry," I reassured her, "I'll be with you just as soon as I've finished this. . .

sentence."

DAD PROBLEM 4: **BATTERY**

LOOK OUT FOR THIS TELL-TALE SIGN:
Your dad just goes on . . . and on . . . and on. . .

LISTEN OUT FOR THESE TELL-TALE SIGNS:
Blah . . . blah . . . blah . . . blah. . .

WHAT CAUSES THE PROBLEM:
Unlike a car battery which goes flat, the
problem with a dad's battery is just the
opposite. A dad's battery is Long Life,
in other words it enables your dad to go on

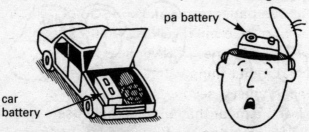

pa battery

car
battery

. . . and on . . . and on. . . So, an innocent
and inoffensive little remark on your part will
set him going on and on. For example:

YOU: "Dad, can I have a 250 megabyte main
frame computer with colour monitor,

joystick, full games pack, CD-Rom and link
up to the Internet? Er . . . please?"
DAD: "You want another computer?"
YOU: "Yes, please. It only costs a few
thousand pounds —"

DAD: "How much? When I was your age I
had to make do with a *Look and Learn
Annual* every Christmas and I had to buy
that myself from the money I earned doing
thirteen paper rounds before school and that
was a twelve mile walk there and fifteen
back my dad never gave me a lift in the car
and another thing we never had central
heating just a secondhand candle in a
broken jam jar that all the family used to
huddle round to try and ward off the frost
bite . . . blah . . . blah . . . blah. . ."

E.I. DADDIO'S EASY STEP-BY-STEP GUIDE TO DEALING WITH THE PROBLEM OF CLASSIC DADS WHO GO ON . . . AND ON . . . AND ON. . .

(1) Take one large balloon.
(2) As your dad starts to speak, hold it in front of his mouth.
(3) As he talks, the balloon will begin to fill with all his hot air!
(4) Now quickly tie the balloon firmly round his middle and under his arm pits. (He won't notice, because he'll be too busy telling you about the bad old good old days.)
(5) Once the balloon is filled, tie the end.
(6) Now watch your dad float up and away, leaving you in peace to watch the telly, use the hall as a roller skating alley, clean your bike in the bath, think of another way of asking him about that new computer etc.

USEFUL SPARES TO CARRY IF YOUR DAD SUFFERS FROM BATTERY PROBLEMS:

A SPARE SET OF PLUGS: To shove in your ears so you don't have to hear what he's drivelling on about. Pardon? I said, TO! SHOVE! IN! YOUR! EARS! Oh never mind, just get on with the next test!

E.I. DADDIO'S ADVANCED DAD HANDLING COURSE: **TEST 4**

QUESTION: What is a dad with battery problems likely to be full of?

TICK BOX

(a) a fund of wonderful stories about his childhood ☐

(b) hot air ☐

(c) polyunsaturates ☐

ANSWERS:

(a) Ah, this is a trick question! If you've ticked this box, it can mean only one thing – you're a dad! Now go and put this book back in your son/daughter's room immediately.

(b) 1 point

(c) No points. Polyunsaturates is what a dad with buttery problems is likely to be full of.

ENTER YOUR NUMBER OF
POINTS HERE IN THIS BOX:

E.I. Daddio's not very secret diary

1600 hours

When the mobile rang again, I heard a voice that sounded vaguely familiar.

"Hello . . . E.I. Daddio Old Crock Doc Extraordinaire. How can I help you?" it said. Then I realized why the voice sounded vaguely familiar – it was mine.

"My name is Willie Woanty," said a voice on the other end of the phone.

"Oh dear, I am sorry," I said.

"It's my dad," he said.

"What's the problem with him?" I asked.

"The problem's not so much with him as with what he's wearing," sighed Willie. Straightaway I knew what the trouble was.

"Your dad's got gear box problems," I said.

DAD PROBLEM 5: **GEAR BOX**

LOOK OUT FOR THIS TELL-TALE SIGN:
Your dad coming down the stairs looking like this:

LISTEN OUT FOR THIS TELL-TALE NOISE: You are standing in the hall, just about to leave to go to your school parents' evening, when you hear a hideous clunking sound.

uncool shirt

embarassing cravat

cringeworthy cardy

gross medallion

tacky socks

ironed jeans with creases

out-of-date slip-ons

WHAT CAUSES THE PROBLEM:

There is obviously something wrong with his gear box – or as it's sometimes known, his wardrobe. To be more precise, there's something wrong with what's inside his wardrobe. To put it in technical terms, car gear boxes have something called synchromesh. Your dad's gear box is more like synchromess. If your dad is a banger, then this problem can be especially serious, because it means he is likely to have at least one woolly cardie in his gear box:

car's gear box

pa's gear box

Even worse off are people whose dads are cod fathers.* These dads always have a kipper tie in their gear box.

*See page 11

If, on the other hand, your dad comes down the stairs looking like this: . . . there is only one explanation. Your dad is none other than Pop-along Cassidy, the famous cowboy.

E.I. DADDIO'S TIPS FOR DEALING WITH YOUR DAD'S GEAR BOX PROBLEMS:

!!! Warning !!!

Whatever you do, don't let your dad look in the mirror. You might think that him seeing how ridiculous he looks will bring him to his senses. However, it is more likely to bring him to his knees, turn any hair he's got left white and leave him a gibbering wreck as he gazes upon the full horror of what he is wearing.

HOW TO GET YOUR DAD A NEW GEAR BOX:

Getting your dad some new gear that's smarter than what he's wearing – without it using up all your pocket money – is easy. All you have to do is to find a field of turnips with a scarecrow in. Anything the scarecrow's wearing is bound to be smarter than your dad's gear.

USEFUL ACCESSORIES IF YOUR DAD NEEDS A NEW GEAR BOX:

A CHROME HUB CAP: very handy if you've got a veteran dad with nothing on top: it'll cover up his shiny dome nicely. What's more, it's bound to be an improvement on the cap he wears already.

E.I. DADDIO'S ADVANCED DAD HANDLING COURSE: **TEST 5**

QUESTION: Match the clothes from these dad's gear boxes to the types of dad that might own them:

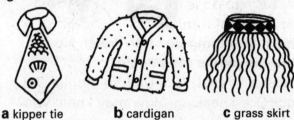

a kipper tie   **b** cardigan   **c** grass skirt

(i) an old banger
(ii) a dad who's GTS (Gone To Seed)
(iii) a cod father

ANSWERS:
a = (iii) He's probably got a herring-bone jacket as well.
b = (i) At least it keeps your Gran busy knitting.
c = (ii) Now you know what the seed he's gone to grows into.

1 point for each correct pair.

ENTER YOUR NUMBER OF POINTS HERE IN THIS BOX:

E.I. Daddio's not very secret diary

1630 hours

I was just settling down to watch Noddy when the phone rang again.

"Hello," I said. "E.I. Daddio Mobile Old Crock Doc speaking. How may I help you?"

"My name's Gail— "

"Not Gail Warning, by any chance?"

"That's right!"

"I rather guessed it might be."

"It's my dad. He's fishing around for something."

"He's not a codfather is he?"

"No. I mean, he keeps trying to look in my room."

The problem with Gail's father was obvious.

"Ah. I think I know what the problem is, Gail."

"You do?"

"Yes, it's staring you right in front of your face. Or rather more accurately, it's staring you right in front of your dad's face."

DAD PROBLEM 6: **HOOTER**

LOOK OUT FOR THIS TELL-TALE SIGN:
On an old crock car, you find the hooter on the door. With an old crock dad, you find the hooter peering *round* the door – the door to your room, that is.

old car's hooter

old pa's hooter

LISTEN OUT FOR THIS TELL-TALE NOISE:
You might hear your dad go Parp! Parp! but more likely you'll see him go Peep! Peep! into your bedroom when he thinks you're not looking.

WHAT CAUSES THE PROBLEM:
It's obvious really: your dad's noticed how good you've been getting at handling him, so he is desperate to get his hands on this book! So much so that he has even ignored the polite notice you've pinned on your bedroom door!*

*See page 21. Unless you've already stuck it up on your bedroom door – in which case see your bedroom door!

E.I. DADDIO'S SOLUTIONS TO THE HOOTER PROBLEM:

FIRST SOLUTION –
USE A TOE ROPE:
Simply tie a length
of rope across
your doorway.
When your dad
next peeps into
your room, his toe
will stumble up against
it and he will trip over
onto his hooter. This will stop
him peeping, but not parping.

DISADVANTAGE OF USING A TOE ROPE:
Unfortunately, as you go racing up the stairs
to your room, to read the next bit of *How To
Handle Your Dad*, in
your excitement you
are likely to forget
that you've set up
the toe rope,
so you will be
tripped up too.

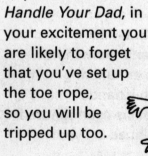

SECOND SOLUTION – HIDE THIS BOOK:
Without further ado, and definitely without
father ado – I mean he's the last person you
want discovering all the important
information between these pages – you must
hide this book. It's a good idea to keep it
some place where your dad
never looks, like his wallet.

That's right, his wallet.
Think about when you ask for
a pocket money rise. He always says, "No, I
haven't got the money." But does he ever
look in his wallet to check? Of course not.

However, if your dad is one of those who
actually keeps a padlock on their wallet and
you haven't got a key, your best bet is to opt
for the simplest solution of all and disguise
this book as a slice of pizza.

All you need to do is to cut out the next
page and stick it on the front cover of this
book. Now colour in the olives black, tomato
bits red, and the cheesy bits yellow. Add
plenty of pepper, so that your dad can't get
too close without sneezing. However, to
make doubly sure he doesn't actually try and
eat this book-disguised-as-pizza, it's a good
idea to colour some of the corner bits in
grey, so that he thinks it's a slice of mouldy
pizza.

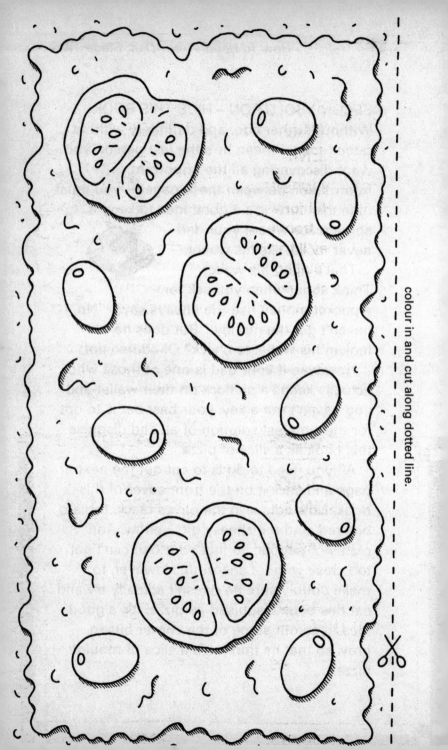

colour in and cut along dotted line.

A USEFUL TOOL TO HAVE IF YOUR DAD HAS A HOOTER PROBLEM:

MONKEY WRENCH: a monkey is very useful for wrenching your dad away from your bedroom door. They'll try all manner of tricks eg pulling your dad's shoe laces undone, swinging from the chandelier in the hall, jumping off the top of the door onto your dad's head. Of course, it *will* be a wrench for your dad, but he'll just have to call a halt to his search for your copy of *How To Handle Your Dad*, while he deals with the monkey.

E.I. DADDIO'S ADVANCED DAD HANDLING COURSE: **TEST 6**

Fill in the right words in the gaps:

YOUR . . . . .'S HOOTER GOES . . . . . WHEN IT . . . . . AROUND YOUR BEDROOM DOOR AND THAT REALLY GIVES YOU THE . . . . .

PARP   **PEEPS**   **PIP**   **POP**

ANSWER:

YOUR **POP'S** HOOTER GOES **PARP** WHEN IT
PEEPS AROUND YOUR BEDROOM DOOR
AND THAT REALLY GIVES YOU THE **PIP**.

One point for pop one point for parp one
point for peep and one point for pip.

ENTER YOUR NUMBER OF
POINTS HERE IN THIS BOX:

E.I. Daddio's not very secret diary

1700 hours
I was just
climbing
out of my
van —

— when I spotted a figure.

I recognized it immediately. It was
0898 100100

My phone number. It was on the side of
my van. Then I noticed another familiar
figure, running towards me. It was a regular
customer of mine: Seeta Down.

"How are you Seeta?" I asked her.

"I'm . . . hah . . . I'm . . . hah . . . out . . .
hah . . . of . . . hah . . . puff, " she gasped.

"Here. Have one of mine," I said, digging
deep into a box in my bag of shopping.

"It's a sugar puff."

No sooner had I given Seeta
a sugar puff, than another
figure came bounding
round the corner.

"Seeta! What do you think
you're doing?" he yelled.

"It's my dad!" cried Seeta.

"You've got a problem
with your dad Seeta," I said. "A serious
problem known to all mobile Old Crock Docs
as 'running on'!"

DAD PROBLEM 7: **RUNNING ON**

LOOK OUT FOR THIS TELL-TALE SIGN:
Your dad runs after you when you don't want him to.

LISTEN OUT FOR THESE TELL-TALE NOISES:
".................... (INSERT YOUR NAME HERE) what do you think you're doing with my
(a) electric drill (b) silk dressing gown
(c) Rolling Stones CD set?"

WHAT CAUSES THE PROBLEM:
For some unfathomable reason, your dad seems to find it totally unreasonable that you are trying to borrow his (a) electric drill for a game of Robodentist II (b) his silk dressing gown to take your bike to bits on, to save making the front room carpet dirty (c) his Rolling Stones CD set because you've lost your frisbee.

E.I. DADDIO'S SOLUTION TO RUNNING ON PROBLEMS:

Remove your dad's fan belt. That way, he'll be too busy trying to hold his trousers up to run on after you.

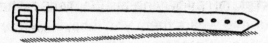

USEFUL TOOL TO HAVE IF YOU HAVE A DAD WHO'S RUNNING ON:

WHEEL BRACES: Wheel braces for old crock cars look like this:

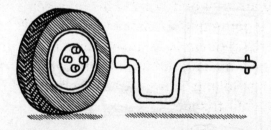

Wheel braces for old crock pas look like this:

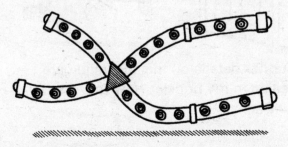

If you can get a pair of wheel braces for your dad for Christmas or his birthday, the benefits will be enormous. Firstly, your dad will be touched: by you that is, when you ask him for some dosh to buy your mum's Christmas present as you've spent all your pocket money buying his. Secondly, when your dad wears them you'll have no more running on problems with him. All you need to do, when you suspect your dad is about to run on after you, is to make sure the back of his wheel braces are hooked round a door handle. Then, as your dad starts running, the wheel braces will s-t-r-e-t-c-h until they eventually ping him back to the door.

Further details on this technique are revealed in my booklet *How to Door Handle Your Dad.*

E.I. DADDIO'S ADVANCED DAD
HANDLING COURSE: **TEST 7**

QUESTION 1 Match the following things that you are trying to borrow from your dad with what you are trying to borrow them for:

(a) electric drill
(b) his Rolling Stones CD set
(c) his silk dressing gown

(i) to replace your lost frisbee
(ii) for a game of Robodentist II
(iii) to take your bike to bits on

QUESTION 2 Match these tell-tale noises to the dad problems with which they are associated:

(a) Grrrr!   (i) wet plugs
(b) blah!   (ii) hooter
(c) peep   (iii) overheating
(d) slurp   (iv) battery

ANSWERS:

1: (a) = (ii); (b) = (i); (c) = (iii)

1 point for each correct pair.

2: (a) = (iii); (b) = (iv); (c) = (ii); (d) = (i)

Take one point for each correct answer, but be careful where you put it, because they're very sharp.

ENTER YOUR NUMBER OF
POINTS HERE IN THE BOX

How To Handle Your Dad : Stage Three

YOUR E.I. DADDIO ADVANCED DAD HANDLING COURSE TEST RESULTS:

Add up your total points for each test here:

	MY POINTS	TOTAL POSSIBLE POINTS
TEST 1	☐	2
TEST 2	☐	4
TEST 3	☐	1
TEST 4	☐	3
TEST 5	☐	3
TEST 6	☐	4
TEST 7	☐	7
MY TOTAL	☐	POSSIBLE TOTAL **24**

WHAT YOUR SCORE MEANS:

More than 24: You obviously didn't manage to get your dad to help you with your maths homework. Go out and buy a copy of *Dippy and Drippy's Very First Book of Really Easy Little Adding Up Sums for the Under Fours*.

Between 1 and 23: You are well on your way to becoming an expert Old Crock Doc. Don't get ideas above your station, though. I mean, you never know when there might be a train coming.

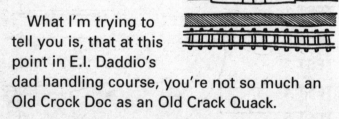

What I'm trying to tell you is, that at this point in E.I. Daddio's dad handling course, you're not so much an Old Crock Doc as an Old Crack Quack.

Less than 1: You've obviously been wearing a woolly vest in June and the heat's gone to your brain. Well, it would've done if you had one, which given your score seems very unlikely.

How To Handle Your Dad : Stage Four

E.I. DADDIO'S DAD CIRCUIT DIAGRAM

Just copy the words at the bottom of the page describing various bits of your dad, into the right boxes:

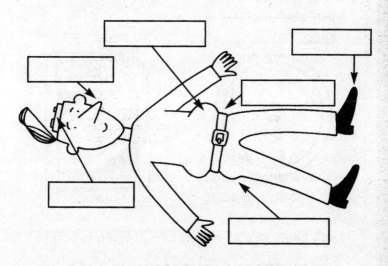

HOOTER   **BACK SEAT**   **FAN BELT**
SPARE TYRE   **BOOT**   **BATTERY**

How To Handle Your Dad : Stage Five

TOOLS, SPARES AND ACCESSORIES CHECK LIST:

Just copy the words at the bottom of the page describing various spares, tools and accessories into the right boxes:

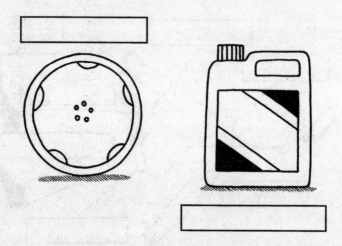

**HOSEPIPE   CHROME HUB CAPS
SPARE YES-U-CAN   MONKEY WRENCH
WHEEL BRACES   TOE ROPE
PLUGS (FOR YOUR EARS)**

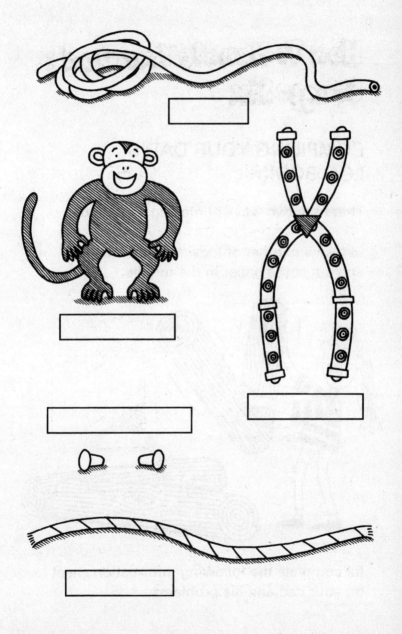

How To Handle Your Dad :
Stage Six

COMPILING YOUR DAD'S
LOG BOOK

There are two ways of making a log book.

(i) take a number of logs, fold them in half and put some paper in the middle.

(ii) complete the following information sheet on your dad and his problems.

DAD'S LOG BOOK

YOUR NAME . . . .

YOUR DAD'S NAME . . . .

PART 1:
BASIC MECHANICAL DADA-TA:

DATE YOUR DAD WAS BUILT . . . .

DATE(S) YOUR DAD WAS REBUILT . . . .

. . . .

DAD TYPE: VINTAGE / VETERAN / CLASSIC /
AS APPROPRIATE*

PART 2:
DAD PROBLEMS:

1: OVERHEATING

DATE YOUR DAD OVERHEATED . . . . . . 199_

NUMBER OF CUPS OF TEA YOU HAD TO
MAKE HIM BEFORE HE COOLED DOWN
. . . . (to the nearest 100)

NUMBER OF TIMES YOU HAD TO LISTEN
TO HIS BEATLES CD BEFORE HE COOLED
DOWN . . . . (to the nearest 1000)

LENGTH OF TIME YOU HAD TO LEAVE HIM
IN THE COLD SHOWER BEFORE HE COOLED
DOWN . . . . HOURS . . . . MINUTES

*Delete as appropriate; or vintage, veteran or classic for that matter.

2: GETTING STARTED

DATE YOUR DAD WOULDN'T START

. . . . 199_

WHAT IT TOOK TO WIND HIM UP

YOUR GRAN COMING TO STAY   YES/NO
YOUR NEIGHBOUR'S CHAIN SAW   YES/NO
MAN UNITED'S AWAY STRIP   YES/NO

YOUR GRAN DRESSING UP IN HER
MAN UNITED AWAY STRIP AND
THREATENING YOUR NEIGHBOUR
WITH HIS CHAIN SAW   YES/NO

3: WET PLUGS

DATE YOUR DAD DEVELOPED WET PLUGS

. . . . 199_

HOW HIGH YOU HAD TO JUMP LIKE A JIVE
BUNNY BEFORE HE DRIED OFF

. . . . METRES

4: BATTERY

DATE YOUR DAD'S BATTERY WOULDN'T
RUN OUT . . . . 199_

DATE YOUR DAD GOT BACK FROM HIS
BALLOON TRIP (IF INDEED HE IS BACK)
. . . . 199_

5: GEAR BOX

DATE YOU FINALLY GAVE UP ON YOUR
DAD'S GEAR BOX . . . . 199_

YOUR DAD'S CHEST SIZE . . . .

INSIDE LEG . . . .

SHOE SIZE . . . .

(Keep this information
handy, just in case you are
passing any turnip fields
with likely-looking
scarecrows in.)

6: HOOTER

DATE YOUR DAD STARTED PEEPING

. . . . 199_

DATE YOUR DAD STARTED PARPING

. . . . 199_

DATE YOU BOUGHT YOUR MONKEY

. . . . 199_

YOUR MONKEY'S NAME . . . .

DATE YOU HAD TO BUY A CHANDELIER
OUT OF YOUR POCKET MONEY

. . . . 199_

7: RUNNING ON

DATE YOUR DAD STARTED RUNNING ON
AFTER YOU . . . . 199_

DISTANCE HE CAN TRAVEL BEFORE HIS
WHEEL BRACES PING HIM BACK

. . . . METRES

It was another dark and stormy night. . .

and I was working hard at my desk, when I
was suddenly woken up by a strange ringing
in my left ear. It was the telephone. As
you've probably guessed by now, I'm always
going to sleep with my telephone in my ear.

"Is that you, Daddio?" asked the voice at the other end. "Indeedio it is. Who is that?"

"Your publisher, Algernon Twistleton-Smythe. Don't you recognize my voice?"

"Er . . . not when it's written down, no," I admitted.

"What does your watch say?" asked my publisher.

"Umm . . . let me see. Oh yes, Rolex," I replied.

"I mean, it's New Year's Eve and it's one minute to midnight. You've got sixty seconds to finish your book on *How To Handle Your Dad*!"

"No, no that's not right," I said. "I've got fifty four seconds to finish my book on *How To Handle Your Dad*. But don't worry, I'm almost at the end of the book."

"Grrr!" said my publisher, sounding very much like an overheating vintage dad, "And I'm almost at the end of my tether."

"Can't you send out for another one?" I suggested.

"Look," said Algernon Twistleton-Smythe. He sounded frantic. "The problems I'm having with my dad are driving me crazy! There's smoke coming out from under his bonnet, I asked him for more pocket money but he won't budge, he's been singing "Bridge Over Troubled Water" to my mum since tea time, he's just going on and on, wearing a really dreadful tie, trying to peer into my room and, oh no . . . I think he's trying to run after me, just because he knows I'm on the phone to you!"

"I'm afraid I simply must stay here and finish the book, but I'll send one of my apprentices along. They've just been reading the book and are really quite expert Old Crock Docs by now."

"All right, but hurry. . .!"

Go on! That's right, you! You should be able to work out the problems my publisher is having with his dad. Get round to his place would you? His address is in the front of the book.

Thanks. Now with any luck, by the time you get back I'll have finished typing the last

PAGE.

How To Handle Your Mum

By Roy Apps

Illustrated by Nick Sharratt

PONY

Hippo

Scholastic Children's Books,
Commonwealth House, 1-19 New Oxford Street,
London WC1A 1NU, UK

A division of Scholastic Ltd
London ~ New York ~ Toronto ~ Sydney ~ Auckland
Mexico City ~ New Delhi ~ Hong Kong

Published in this edition by Scholastic Ltd, 2002

First published in the UK by Scholastic Ltd, 1994
Text copyright © Roy Apps, 1994
Illustrations copyright © Nick Sharratt, 1994

ISBN 0 439 98230 8

!!! Warning !!!

The information contained in this book can be highly dangerous if it falls into the wrong hands, i.e. your mum's.

   To prevent this from happening you should take one of the following precautions:

1 Memorise every word in the book and then eat it.*ᵛ
2 If you are a girl, disguise the nature of this book by cutting out the next page and sticking it on the cover.
3 If you are a boy, disguise the nature of this book by cutting out the next page but one and sticking it on the cover.

TV cook Kevin Bowtie suggests you try the following recipe if you do decide to eat this book. Extra Whopper Book Burger: *(i) Place book in a stale sesame seed bun. (ii) Place book-filled bun on paper napkin. (iii) Add two tablespoons of extra hot chillies. (iv) Eat (the bun, not the napkin).*

ᵛ *This book is suitable for vegetarians.*

1001 Ways to Become a Perfect Daughter

By Gladys Goodchild

1001 Ways to Become a Perfect Son

My angel!

By Norbert Neverude

Contents

How To Handle Your Mum: Stage One

Why it's important to be able to handle your mum – NOW!

Ask yourself this question:

What's the difference between your mum and a mountain bike with square wheels and 57 reverse gears?

Tricky one, this, so here's a picture to help you.

Look at the gears on that bike – what a laugh!
Now look at the gear on that mum – what an
even bigger laugh! But to get back to the
question: your mum isn't like a mountain
bike with square wheels and 57 gears,
because *you can't take her back to the shop
you got her from and ask them for a model
that's easier to handle*. You've got to learn to
handle the mum you got when you were
born.

We regret mums cannot be exchanged

It's important to be able to handle your
mum *now*, because the older you get, the
more difficult it becomes. In fact, the only
people who don't need to learn how to
handle their mums are newborn babies.
They've got it (or rather her) completely and
absolutely worked out. Take the following
scenes. Done that? Now put them back in the
book and read them!

Scene 1
YOU: *(Slamming the front door behind you
and yelling at the top of your voice)* Hey,
Mum! *Mum!!!* I wanna Coke!
YOUR MUM: Come back in again like
a civilised human being, speak properly
and remember the little word . . .

YOU: *(Coming in again, this time closing the door quietly and speaking in hushed tones)* Mum? Could I have a Coke, please?
YOUR MUM: No, you can't. We're just about to have dinner.
(*Result:* You don't get your Coke.)

Scene 2

NEWBORN BABY: *(Hammering fists on Mum's chest)* Yahhh!!!! Bahhhh!!! Woooo!!!! YEEAAAGHHH!!!
MUM: Ooo . . . my little darling. Do you want a drink?
(*Result:* Baby gets a drink.)

Scene 3

It is half past nine in the morning. You are lying down on your bed, taking a well-earned, post-breakfast rest, kind of half-dozing, half-daydreaming about how much better your life will be when you finally become a World-Beating Number One Sports Superstar. Suddenly a hurricane blasts into the room. It's –

YOUR MUM: Oh, for goodness' sake, *(insert your name here)*! Get up, you great schlummock and go and do something useful like learning to play the clarinet or hoovering your room or visiting your grandmother. (*Result:* Either you learn to play the clarinet, tidy up your room and visit your grandmother, or you reach a compromise and learn how to hoover up your grandmother with a clarinet.)

WOOSH!

Scene 4

It is half past nine in the morning. The newborn baby is lying down in its cot, taking a well-earned rest, half-dozing, half-daydreaming under its Spot the Dog mobile. Suddenly a kind and gentle breeze wafts into the room. It is –

MUM: Aaahhhh . . . Does my little darling want to go to sleepy-byes?
(*Sings*) Bye, Baby Bunting, etc., etc.

14

(*Result:* Baby is left on his/her own to do whatever he/she wants until it's time for another drink. [See Scene 2.])

So there you have it. There are two methods open to you of handling your mum. Either you can go back to being a baby again and start wearing nappies, or you can read this book. Which method do you fancy? Tricky decision, eh? You probably need two seconds to decide. So here they are:

ONE SECOND	ANOTHER SECOND

Made your choice? OK, for those of you who have decided to become babies again, I hope you'll have a nappy time! Don't forget you'll need a dummy too. On second thoughts, you won't need a dummy, because you probably *are* one.

For those incredibly intelligent and sensible people who have decided to learn how to handle their mums by reading this book, the first thing you must do is this: TURN OVER!

How To Handle Your Mum: Stage Two

Finding out just what kind of mum you've got

Just what kind of mum have you got? There's a very simple answer to this, which is – How on earth do you expect *me* to know? You've never even introduced me to her.

There are only three kinds of mums who are easy to cope with. And there aren't many of them left. These mums are rather like blue whales and African elephants, in other words they are an endangered species.*

Type 1: The Mummy-Type Mum
An incredibly ancient mum originating from North-East Africa and known as an Ancient Egyptian Mummy.

---

* According to wildlife expert, Dr David Bellamummy.

They look like this:
If your mum is this
kind of mummy, I've
only got one thing to
say to you: I hope you
take after your dad!

**(Typical Mummy-Moan:
"Have you been cleaning
your bike chain in the
kitchen sphinx *again?*")**

Type 2: The Mother-
Type Mum
A mum who thinks
she's the best thing
since Super Nintendo
and who therefore
likes to be called
Mother or, more
correctly, *Mother
Superior.* They look
like this:

If your mum looks like this, tell her to stop
buying her clothes from the local convent's
jumble sales.

(Typical Mother-Superior Saying: Nun.)

Type 3: The Mama-Type Mum
Mums who are dead posh like
to be called Mama
(pronounced Mar-Mar), which
is short for Mar-Ma-Ladies.
They look like this.
If your mum is one of these
Mar-Ma-Ladies, she will be
very easy to handle. Just keep
her on the top shelf in the
larder and only bring her out
at meal times.

**(Typical Mar-Ma-Lady Saying: "Use a
spoon to get me out of the jar, not a
knife!")**

The chances are that your mum is neither an
Ancient Egyptian, nor a nun, nor a jar of
orange jam, so learning how to handle her is
going to be rather like conjuring, in other
words, a very *tricky* business.

Fortunately, help is at hand. To be more
precise, help is *in* your hand in the form of
this book. For the first time in the history of
mankind – and more importantly of *mum*kind
– a giant mainframe computer has been

designed to provide answers to some of the most difficult problems people have with their mums. It's called the MUMBO (stands for MUMs had Better watch Out) JUMBO.

Now, it's a well-known scientific fact that mums aren't like any other sort of people. So first of all, an incredibly brilliant computer programmer* fed millions of megabytes of data into the MUMBO JUMBO to try to discover what kind of mum I had. After spending years reading the data, the MUMBO JUMBO eventually flashed this message up on the screen:

FIRST OF ALL
FIND OUT
WHAT PLANET
SHE IS FROM

---

* This incredibly brilliant computer programmer is also incredibly modest and won't reveal his name.
However, you can find out who he is by rearranging the following letters: E M.

I fell off my seat. I was stunned. (This was because I banged my head on the desk.)

"First of all find out what planet she's from?" I said.

FOR GOODNESS' SAKE, STOP REPEATING EVERYTHING I SAY...

YOUR MUM IS AN ALIEN

"Are you sure?" I asked.

OF COURSE I'M SURE, BIRD BRAIN. WHAT MAKES YOU THINK YOU'RE DIFFERENT FROM ANYONE ELSE?

IF YOU DON'T BELIEVE ME TRY THIS QUESTIONNAIRE...

How To Handle Your Mum: Stage Three

Finding out if your mum is an alien

Complete the following questionnaire to find out what kind of alien your mum is.

1. Does your mum ever say (or think) any of the following to you:
a) "I think you . . .
☐ . . . watch too much telly."
☐ . . . have far too much pocket money."
☐ . . . go to bed far too late."

21

b) "I don't think you . . .
☑ . . . get enough homework."
☐ . . . understand the meaning of tidiness."
☐ . . . eat enough cabbage."

2. Does your mum think Sonic the Hedgehog is:
☐ a kiddie's cartoon series
☑ your favourite band
☐ a small prickly creature who lives at the bottom of your garden?

3. Does your mum think any of the following are the height of fashion?
☐ school blazers
☐ anoraks
☑ hand-knitted pullovers
☐ vests?

22

4. Does your mum reckon any of the following people are right on/cool/well smart?

☒ Cilla Black

☐ The woman who reads The News (any of them)

☐ The bloke who reads The News (any of them)

☐ Seb Coe?

If you've ticked any one of the above questions, then ask yourself, *where on earth* has your mum been living for the past five years?

To which the answer must be . . . *nowhere on earth*. Therefore she must be an alien.

To which there is a very obvious question . . . "Which planet does she come from?"

To which there is a very obvious answer . . . "Ma(r)s."

How To Handle Your Mum: Stage Four

What makes mums different?

Once I'd discovered that my mum was an alien, a lot of things began to fall into place. Like why she calls my dad "Hunkikins" when she thinks I'm not listening, when really his name is Eric. ("Hunkikins" is obviously the alien translation of Eric.) But that still didn't explain just why mums are *so* difficult to handle. I asked the MUMBO JUMBO to explain.

And the MUMBO JUMBO said:

ALIEN OR HUMAN,
MUMS ARE
DIFFERENT

So I asked the MUMBO JUMBO what it is that makes mums different from other aliens and humans.

And the MUMBO JUMBO said:

MUMS HAVE **CHILDREN***

I said, "Could've told *you* that!"
And the MUMBO JUMBO replied:

WELL YOU DIDN'T. SO THERE!

I asked the MUMBO JUMBO *why* having children made mums different.

And the MUMBO JUMBO replied:

ATCHOOOO!!!

---

* In case you were thinking, "What about dads?", dads don't have *children*. They just acquire them once they are born.

The **MUMBO JUMBO** had obviously got a computer virus. So I put it to bed with a mug of hot honey and lemon and when it felt better it said this:

When they are going to have a baby, mums get cravings for strange mixtures of foods: eg brussels sprouts with custard, or chocolate flake coated in luscious cold brown gravy, or tomato sauce and prune trifle, or Extra Big Whoppa Burgers, or – Excuse me, I feel sick.

AAATCHOOO! I'VE GOT THAT VIRUS BACK AGAIN. CAN I GO BACK TO SLEEP UNTIL THE NEXT CHAPTER?

So I said, "OK."

How to Handle Your Mum: Stage Four

And the MUMBO
JUMBO said:

ZZZZZZZZZZZZZZ

I said, "Wake up!"
And the MUMBO
JUMBO said:

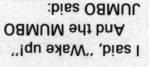

YOU SAID I COULD
GO TO SLEEP
UNTIL THE
NEXT CHAPTER!

I said, "This *is* the
next chapter."

And the MUMBO
JUMBO said:

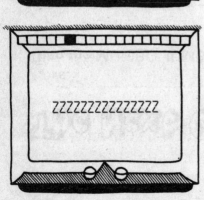

OH NO IT ISN'T!

So I said, "Oh, yes it . . .

The Next Chapter

. . . is."

Then the MUMBO JUMBO said:

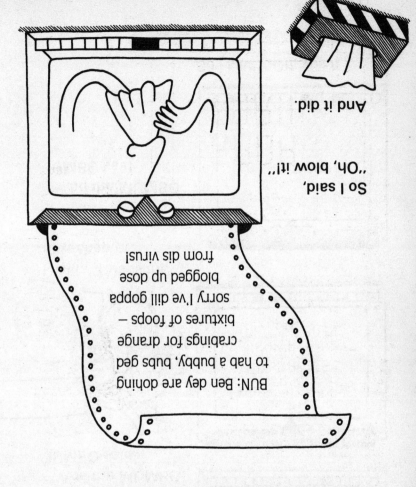

BUN: Ben dey are dohing
to hab a bubby, bubs ged
crabings for drange
bixtures of foops —
sorry I've dill goppa
blogged up dose
from dis virus!

So I said,
"Oh, blow it!"

And it did.

And this is what it said next:

"Yes, we know all that."

"Pardon? I didn't quite catch that . . ."

WHEN THEY'RE GOING TO HAVE A BABY, MUMS GET CRAVINGS FOR STRANGE MIXTURES OF FOODS —

EATING THESE STRANGE MIXTURES OF FOOD GIVES MUMS CERTAIN SUPERHU-*mum* POWERS. ALL MUMS HAVE AT LEAST ONE OF THESE SUPERHU-*mum* POWERS. THE MOST COMMON OF THESE SUPERHU-*mum* POWERS IS RADAR EAR —

RADAR EAR!!!!

How To Handle Your Mum: Stage Five

The five superhu-mum powers and how to combat them

1 Radar Ear

What is Radar Ear?

I pressed the keypad on my mouse to see what information the MUMBO JUMBO had on mums with Radar Ear. Very quickly it said:

ERROR!!
ERROR!!
ERROR!!

Then it said:

ARRGHH!!!!!!!
GET THAT THING
AWAY FROM ME!!

And I suddenly realised what the problem
was. The MUMBO JUMBO was scared of my
mouse. It leapt up onto the top shelf of my
bookcase and there it stayed. Luckily I've got
a back-up computer. It's called My Brain. So
here is everything I know about mums with
Radar Ear.

An ordinary ear looks like this:

Ear trumpet

Ear lobe

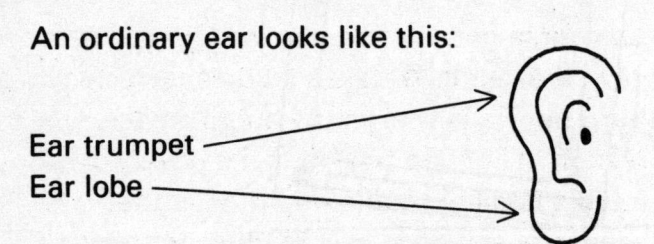

A mum's Radar Ear looks like this:

Satellite dish

Ear stud concealing
special microchip

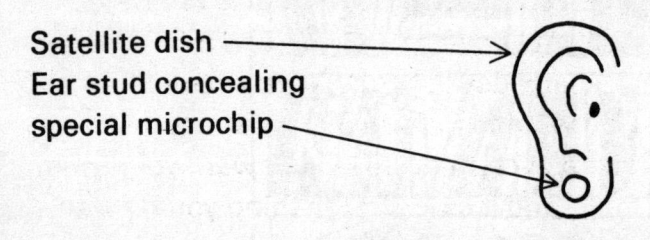

The kind of things mums with Radar Ears
tend to say are:
"*I hear* that the Queen's coming to open the
new by-pass."

Now, did that mum
actually go to
Buckingham Palace
and hear the Queen
say: "Philip! Ay'm
just orff to open the
new Clogbury bay-
pass. Ay've left you a
boil-in-the-bag kipper
for your supper."

Of course not. Rather, she was just about to give the cat its Whiskas when she decided to turn her Radar Ear in the approximate direction of London SW1 and, so powerful is a mum's Radar Ear, she heard what the Queen was saying to Prince Philip without any difficulty whatsoever.

When your mum comes to use her Radar Ear on you, however, it works in a particularly devilish way. It can actually decide what to pick up and what not to. It picks up everything you *don't* want your mum to hear, and it cuts out anything you *do* want her to hear.

I asked the MUMBO JUMBO to explain and it said:

GET RID OF
THAT MOUSE!

So I did. And the MUMBO JUMBO came up
with the following table:

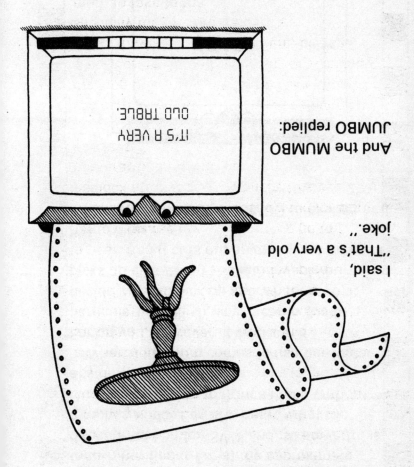

I said,
"That's a very old
joke."

And the MUMBO
JUMBO replied:

IT'S A VERY
OLD TABLE.

Then the MUMBO JUMBO came up with this
table:

Words and phrases of yours that a mum's Radar Ear always picks up	Words and phrases of yours that a mum's Radar Ear never picks up
"*!$!*$!!" (that is, any word that is at all rude.)	"I'd like (a) a 20-gear mountain bike, (b) a horse and stables in the back garden for my birthday, please."
"No, of course my mum won't mind if we look after your pet tarantula for the holidays."	"Can we go to Disneyland for our holiday this year?"
"Chomp, chomp!" (tucking into the Black Forest Gateau that's thawing specially for your mum to take to the school Parents' Association dance.)	"Can Karen and I go to the Take That concert at Wembley Stadium, please?"

You can work out how good your mum's Radar Ear is by conducting the following experiment:

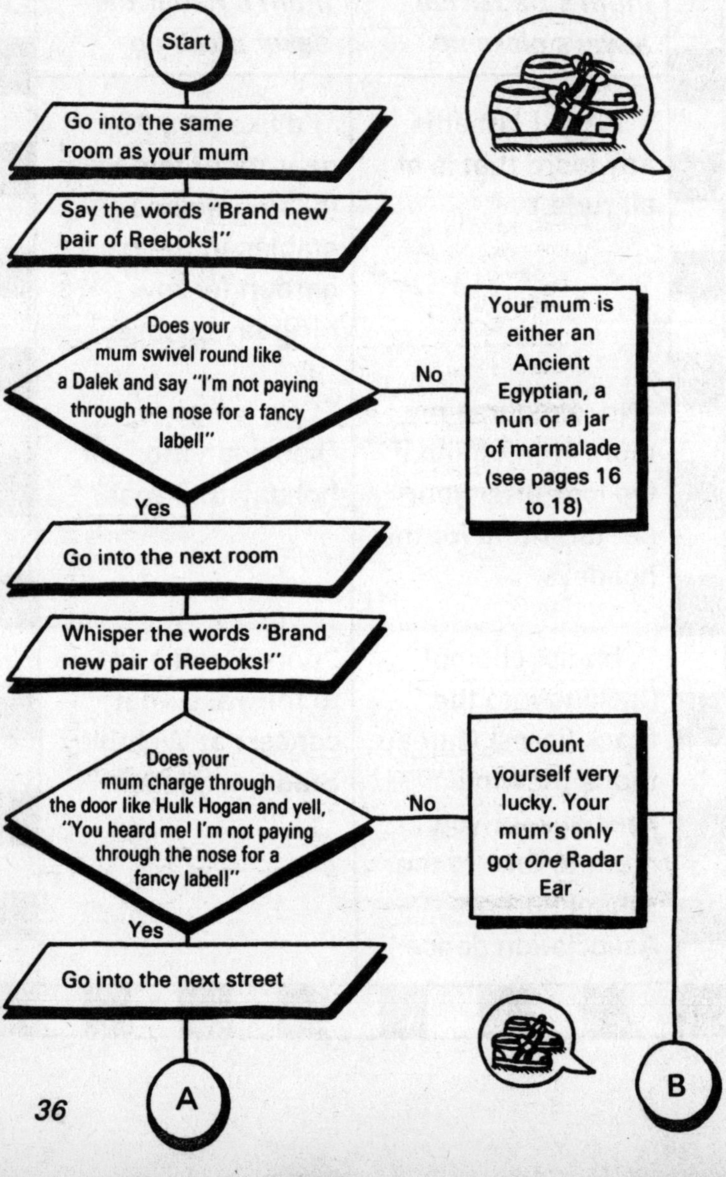

Start

Go into the same room as your mum

Say the words "Brand new pair of Reeboks!"

Does your mum swivel round like a Dalek and say "I'm not paying through the nose for a fancy label!"

No → Your mum is either an Ancient Egyptian, a nun or a jar of marmalade (see pages 16 to 18)

Yes

Go into the next room

Whisper the words "Brand new pair of Reeboks!"

Does your mum charge through the door like Hulk Hogan and yell, "You heard me! I'm not paying through the nose for a fancy label!"

No → Count yourself very lucky. Your mum's only got *one* Radar Ear

Yes

Go into the next street

A

B

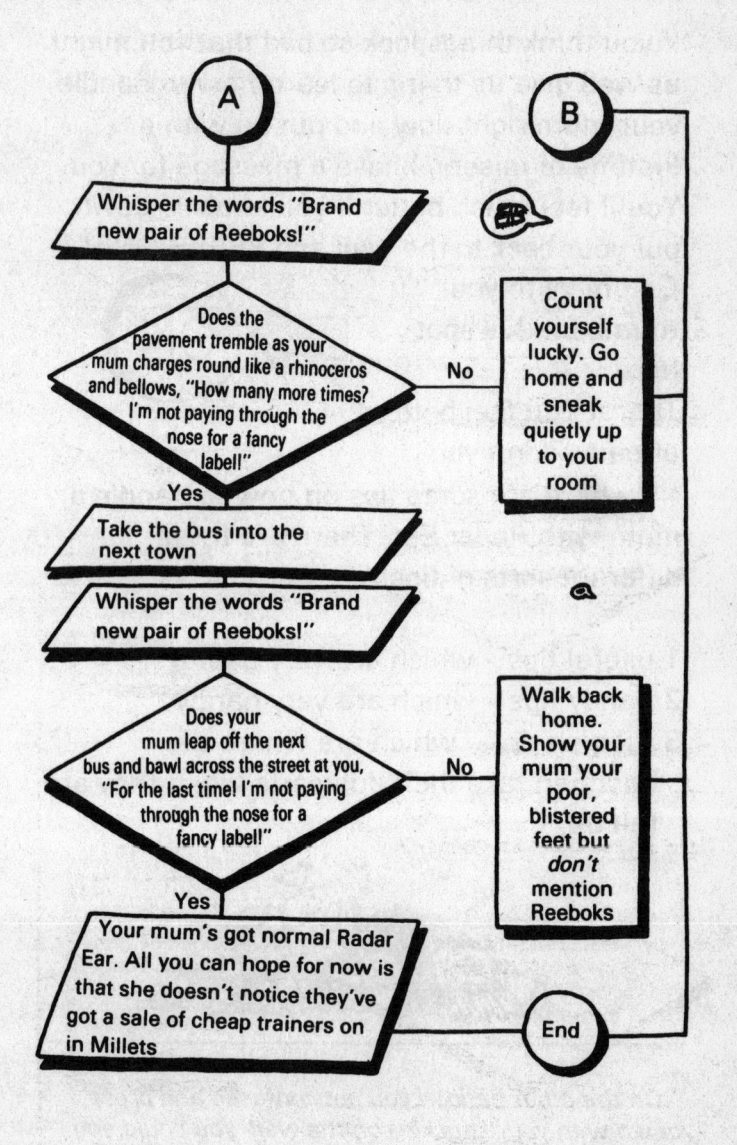

If you think things look so bad that you might as well give up trying to learn how to handle your mum right now and put up with a lifetime of misery, I have a message for you. You'll feel much better if you knuckle down, put your back to the wall and PRESS ON!!*

Go on! With your thumb on this spot here:

There! You feel better already, don't you?

Now here are some tips on how to handle a mum with Radar Ear. There are three different sorts of tips:

1 useful tips – which are very useful
2 handy tips – which are very handy
3 rubbish tips – which are where the dustmen take their dustcarts when they are full up.

---

* On the other hand, if you get confused and press down with your knuckles on the wall, you could end up feeling a lot worse – not to say in need of several bits of sticking plaster.

How to handle mums with Radar Ear

1 The Satellite Solution. Give your mum and her Radar Ear something else to listen to other than you. The most obvious thing to do is to strap her to the chimney, so that her Radar Ear can operate as a satellite dish. I say this is obvious, because if your mum is strapped to the chimney, she certainly will be (obvious, that is).

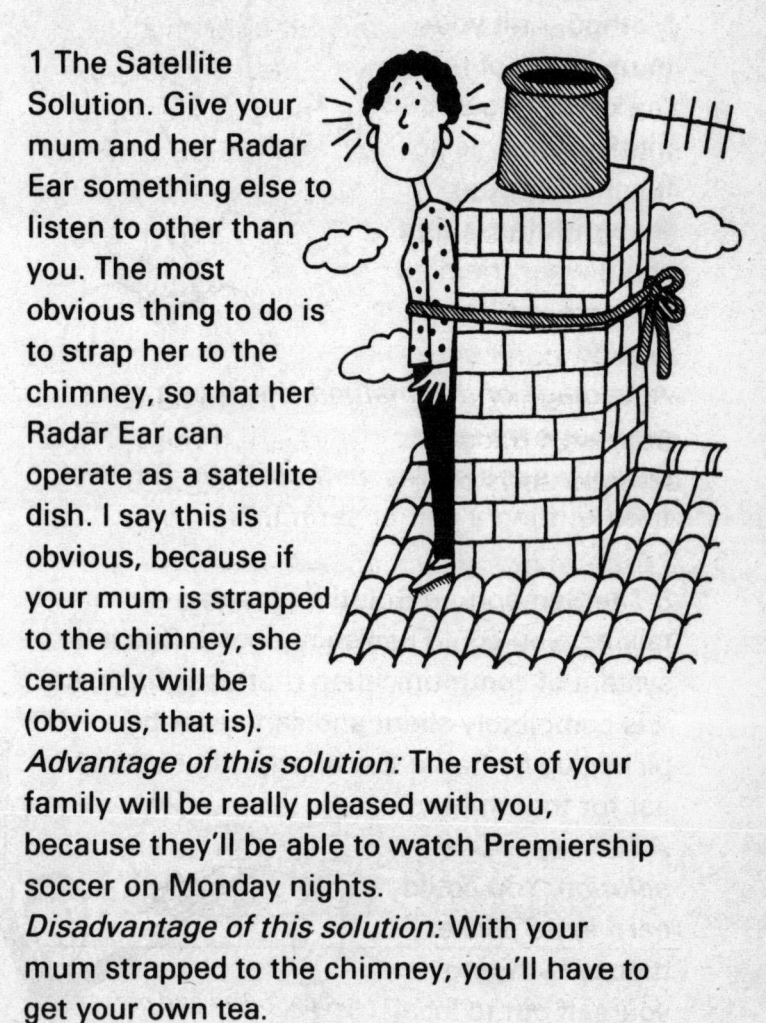

Advantage of this solution: The rest of your family will be really pleased with you, because they'll be able to watch Premiership soccer on Monday nights.

Disadvantage of this solution: With your mum strapped to the chimney, you'll have to get your own tea.

2 The Ear Muff Method. Knit your mum a pair of really thick woolly ear muffs. She'll be so touched by your thoughtfulness that she'll wear them all the time you're around.

Advantage of this method: You won't have to get your own tea.

Disadvantage of this method: Have you ever *tried* knitting a pair of ear muffs?

3 The Semaphore Solution. Instead of talking, you could use semaphore. This is a system of communication that uses flags, so it is completely silent and can never be picked up by Radar Ear or any other sort of ear for that matter.

Advantage of this solution: You could earn extra pocket money by hiring yourself out to local fêtes as a flag pole.

Disadvantage of this solution: Limited as a means of communication – have you ever tried doing semaphore while riding a bike or cleaning your teeth, for example?

wobble!

wobble!

2 Gamma-Ray Eye

What is Gamma-Ray Eye?

ARE YOU
ASKING ME?

asked the MUMBO JUMBO.
"If I am, are you going to tell me the answer?" I replied.

The MUMBO JUMBO said:

So I gave it a silicon chip sandwich.

It took a couple of megabytes and said:

Gamma-Ray Eye enables your mum to actually see *through* things. For example, to anyone else your bed looks like this:

But to a mum with Gamma-Ray Eye, it looks like this:

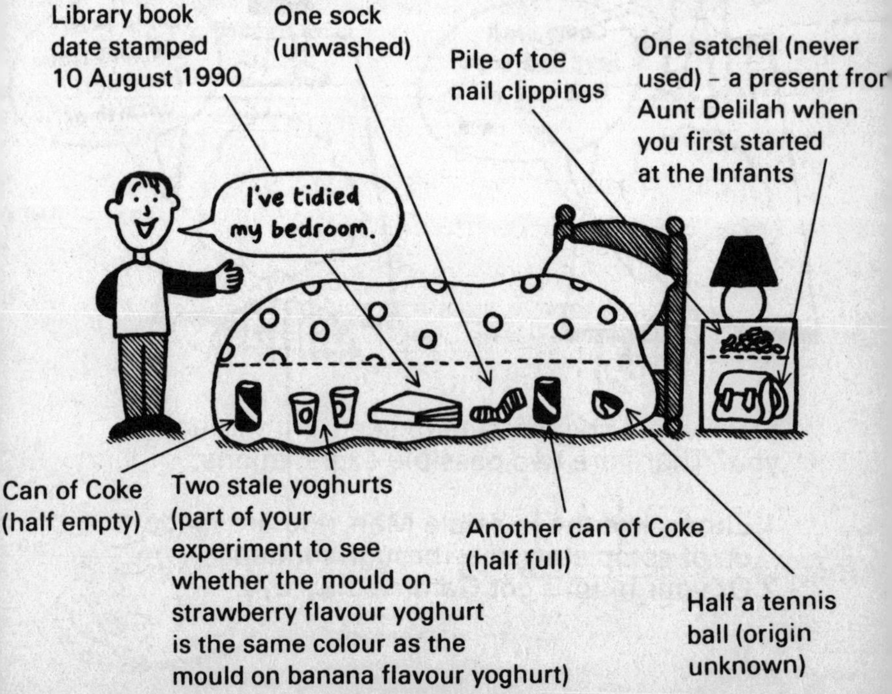

Library book date stamped 10 August 1990

One sock (unwashed)

Pile of toe nail clippings

One satchel (never used) – a present from Aunt Delilah when you first started at the Infants

I've tidied my bedroom.

Can of Coke (half empty)

Two stale yoghurts (part of your experiment to see whether the mould on strawberry flavour yoghurt is the same colour as the mould on banana flavour yoghurt)

Another can of Coke (half full)

Half a tennis ball (origin unknown)

Another problem comes when you're leaving the house. You're halfway to the front door with your back to your mum, but she calls out:

If you're a boy   If you're a girl

Come back here and wipe that egg off your face.

Come back here and clean that nail varnish off.

So how did she manage to see right through you? There are two possible explanations:

1 Either, like the Invisible Man, you are made up of completely see-through matter;
2 Or your mum's got Gamma-Ray Eye.

How to handle mums with Gamma-Ray Eye

"Eh?"

At first I thought the MUMBO JUMBO had suddenly learnt to speak Russian, then I realised this tip on how to deal with Gamma-Ray Eye was so secret, the MUMBO JUMBO would only reveal the details in code. What I needed was a code breaker.

So I looked in the *Yellow Pages* under C for
Code Breakers. It said: *Turn to* Z

I did. And found Zoob Glakers plc, which is
a code for Code Breakers plc. They told me
there were three methods of breaking the
MUMBO JUMBO's code:

1 A stupid way: Hit it hard with a hammer.

2 A hard way: Read it from right to left.

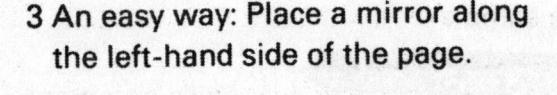

3 An easy way: Place a mirror along
the left-hand side of the page.

OK, readers. Choose your method and break
the code.

HANDLING GAMMA-RAY EYE

IF THERE'S ANYTHING YOU

DON'T WANT YOUR MUM TO SEE

MAKE SURE YOU ARE HOLDING A

MIRROR UP IN FRONT OF HER FACE

What happens, of course, is that the Gamma-Rays are directed straight back at your mum. Elpmis, isn't it?

3 Laser Tongue

What is Laser Tongue?

Sharp, cutting and deadly – that's what a mum's Laser Tongue is. It enables them to come out with really devastating comments. Here are some examples:

(When you've tried to clean your bike by putting it in the dishwasher): "You've got as much brain as a bowl of blancmange."

(When you've asked for the umpteenth time if you can have a pony for your birthday): "Why on earth do we need a pony when we've already got a donkey?" (She means you.)

(When you've just put on your brand new Take That CD): "Oh, no! Sounds like the cat's got trapped in the tumble drier again!"

Laser Tongue works on a Pick 'n' Mix principle. Your mum will pick a target then choose a suitable laser-tongued phrase to describe it. See if you can pick 'n' match these targets to the right Laser Tongue phrase.

Common targets of mums' Laser Tongues	Common phrases of mums' Laser Tongues
Your incredible brain power	about as much use as a chocolate hammer
Your exquisite table manners	two gherkins short of a Big Mac
Your favourite actor/singer	as much taste as a second-hand herbal tea bag
Your superb taste in TV programmes	picked up in the Safari Park
Your keen clothes sense	looks like a herd of wildebeest have just stormed through it
The state of your room	makes a sack of spuds look chic
Your amazing ability to stand on your head for seven and a half minutes without being sick	like Frankenstein's monster, but without his charm

How to handle mums with Laser Tongues

The MUMBO JUMBO said:

And I said, "Any more talk like that, and I'll start using that mouse again!"
So the MUMBO JUMBO said:

I said, "Thank you very much."
Then I realised that this was the MUMBO
JUMBO's handy hint on how to handle your
mum's Laser Tongue. (i.e. be like Ken* and
creep.)

This is how it works:
MUM: Why on earth do we need a pony
when we've got a donkey? (*See above.*)
YOU: Oh, Mum! Why on earth do we need a
pony when we've got a donkey! Oh, how clever
. . .! How witty –
MUM: Do you really think so?
YOU: Oh, yes. Ha, ha, ha! Ho, ho, ho!
MUM: It *was* rather good, now you come to
mention it. Ho, ho, ho!
YOU: Ha, ha, ha! I wish I could
be as witty as that!
MUM: I bet you do! Ho, ho, ho!
YOU: Ha, ha, ha! You *are* going
to let me have a pony, aren't you,
Mum? You're so clever, Mum!
MUM: Yes, of course I am, dear!
YOU: Thank you very much, Mum!

---

* *Full name: Ken-I-do-that-for-you-miss-please-miss,
aka the teacher's pet.*

4 Athlete's Leg

What is Athlete's Leg?

Compared with a mum's speed as she
catches you sneaking out for a game of
football without having first tidied your room,
Linford Christie is about as fast as a snail
with a zimmer frame. Compared with a
mum's speed as she catches you sneaking up
to your room without first having put your
dirty dinner plates in the sink, Sally Gunnell
is about as fast as a tortoise with bricks in its
boots.

Yes, Superhu-mums are *fast*. The really
clever thing, though, is that they don't *look*
fast. That's why it's so easy to be taken by
surprise. It's all to do with clothes.

On top your mum
might look like this:

But *underneath*, she'll
be wearing something
like this:

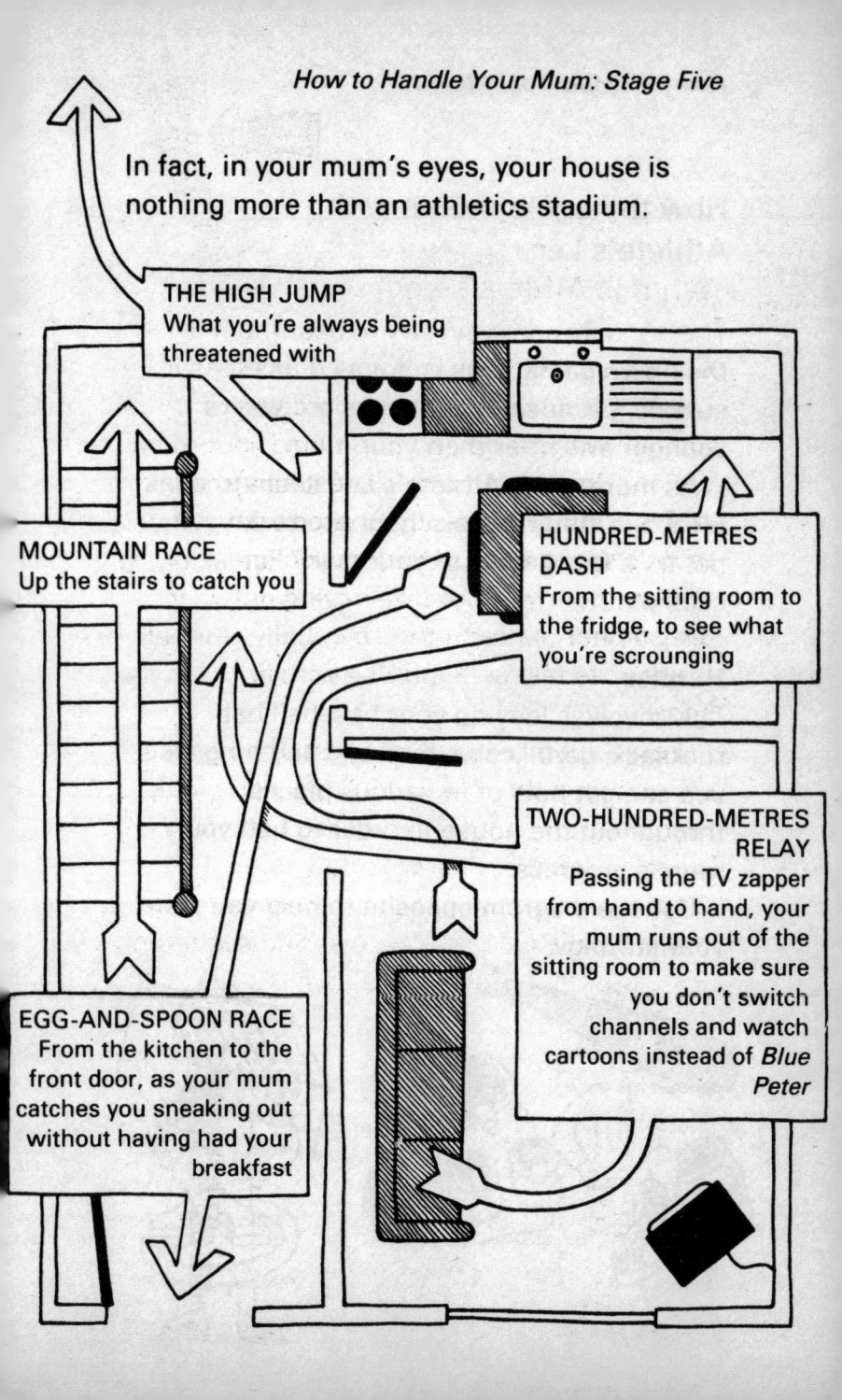

In fact, in your mum's eyes, your house is nothing more than an athletics stadium.

THE HIGH JUMP
What you're always being threatened with

MOUNTAIN RACE
Up the stairs to catch you

HUNDRED-METRES DASH
From the sitting room to the fridge, to see what you're scrounging

TWO-HUNDRED-METRES RELAY
Passing the TV zapper from hand to hand, your mum runs out of the sitting room to make sure you don't switch channels and watch cartoons instead of *Blue Peter*

EGG-AND-SPOON RACE
From the kitchen to the front door, as your mum catches you sneaking out without having had your breakfast

How to handle mums with Athlete's Leg

There's only one way – try to beat them at their own game. This is not as difficult as it sounds, because the chances are you're younger and fitter than your mum.

As mums with Athlete's Leg seem to think life's one continuous school sports day, why not try a few games of your own? For example:

Hurdles

This involves leaving your baseball bat, rucksack, gerbil cage, bike and anything else you can get hold of in various places throughout the house in order to halt your mum's progress.

Use the diagram opposite to help you plan your strategy.

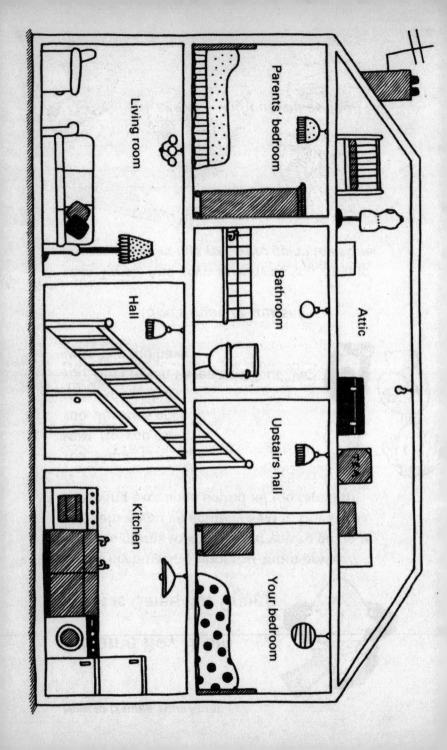

5 Game Boy Brain

What is Game Boy Brain?

This truly amazing Superhu-mum power enables mums to know what you're going to say before you've actually said it. Does the following exchange sound all too familiar?

YOU: Mum . . .
MUM: No, you can't.
YOU: Just this once . . .?
MUM: And no buts.
YOU: But I haven't even said "but" yet!
MUM: Yes you have.

(She's right, of course!)

MUM: Twice. And anyway, why do you want to *(insert whatever it is you were going to ask her for)*

....

....

(See! she knows – without you asking!)

YOU: Oh, go on, Mum! Please! If you let me,
I'll –

*(You're about to say "I'll take the dog for a
walk for you," when your mum butts in.)*

MUM: Dad took it through the car wash
yesterday.

*(Yahoo! Jubilation! You've got her this time,
you think! Her Game Boy Brain has failed
her! She thinks you were going to offer to
wash the car, rather than take the dog for a
walk!)*

YOU: Dad took our dog Rover through the car
wash?
MUM: No, Dad took our car Rover through the
car wash.

YOU: I wasn't going to offer to wash the car, Mum. I was going to offer to take our dog for a walk. That surprised you, didn't it? Eh?

MUM: It certainly did. We haven't got a dog!

(You are about to crawl up to your room, totally and utterly defeated in your request, when your mum strikes the killer blow.)

MUM: OK!

YOU: OK what, Mum?

MUM: You've been very good about the house lately, so I'll let you – just this once. Now run along.

(At this point you realise with a sickening feeling that, what with all the argy-bargying with your mum, you've completely forgotten what it was you'd asked her for in the first place! So you continue crawling up to your room, totally and utterly defeated.)

How to handle mums with Game Boy Brain

I asked the MUMBO JUMBO for advice on this most tricky of all the Superhu-mum powers and it said:

PASS

Which is another way of saying, write the following letter:

Dear Mr Magnusson,
Please could you enter my mum for this year's BBC Mastermind competition. Her chosen subject will be Major Battles of the School Holidays – July the twentieth to September the third.
Yours sincerely

Once entered as a "Mastermind" contestant, your mum will have to start learning to answer questions *after* she has heard them and not before.

FOR YOUR OWN REFERENCE, INSERT
DETAILS OF YOUR MUM'S SUPERHU-MUM
POWERS HERE:

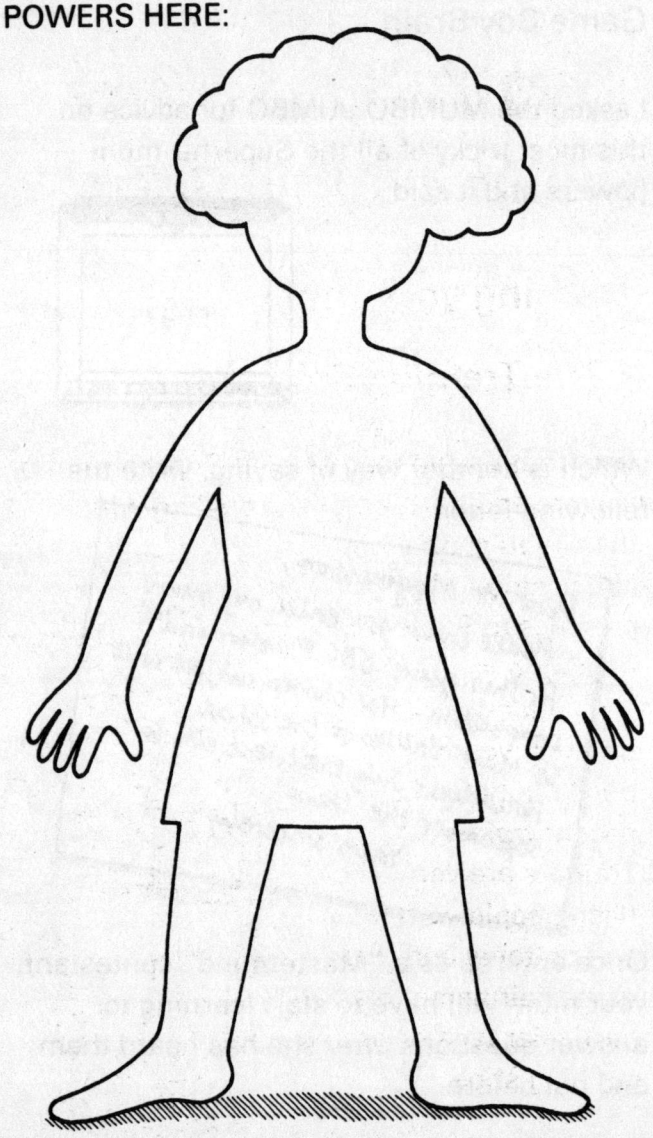

How To Handle Your Mum: Stage Six

Training your mum

1 The Training Program

Now that you've learnt about Superhu-mum powers and have practised dealing with them, you should be in a position to progress to Stage Six – training your mum.

To undertake this training, you will need the help of a decent *trainer*. Trainers are very flash people with fat, soft bottoms and they gave their name to a particular type of running shoe.

However, when I asked the top trainer in the country for his advice on the Training of Mums, he sent me this very *cross* letter. It was:

Then he sent me another very cross letter:

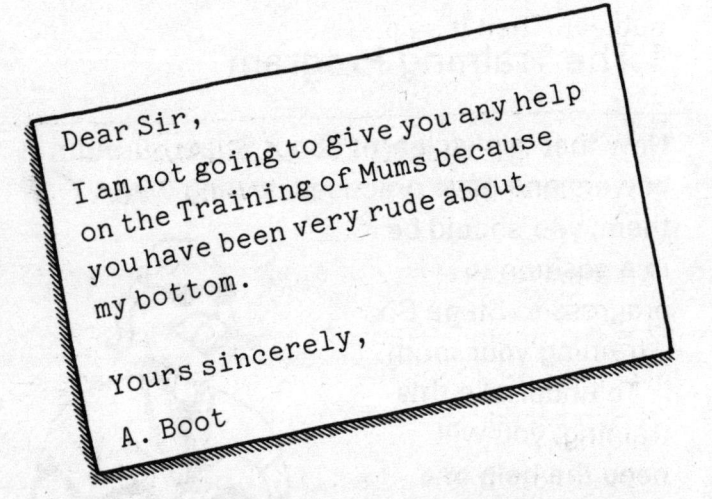

Dear Sir,

I am not going to give you any help on the Training of Mums because you have been very rude about my bottom.

Yours sincerely,

A. Boot

As you probably know, there is only one thing to do if you can't get hold of a decent trainer, and that is to get hold of a decent flip-flop.

However, because of a misunderstanding in the shop, I ended up not with a flip-flop, but a flippy-floppy.

So I loaded it into the MUMBO JUMBO.

And the MUMBO JUMBO said:

OOOOO!!!!
HE-HE-HE
!!!!

Obviously, the training of mums is a ticklish subject. Then it said:

THE TRAINING PROGRAM:
COMPLETE THE FOLLOWING DATA:

1 Is your mum older than you?　　　　YES/NO

2 Is your mum a woman?　　　　　　YES/NO
If your answer to both of the above questions is
YES, proceed:*

3 Does your mum expect you to go to bed
(a) before the Ten o'Clock News
(b) after the Ten o'Clock News
(c) before *Emmerdale?*

** If your answer to either Question 1 or Question 2 is
NO, then contact one of the Sunday newspapers
immediately and offer to sell them your story for a
huge sum of money.*

4 During school holidays, does your mum let you stay in bed until
(a) lunchtime
(b) *Home and Away* time
(c) sunset?

5 You're off school sick. You ask your mum if you can watch TV. Does she say
(a) If you're too ill to go to school, you're too ill to watch telly
(b) Yes, but only schools telly
(c) Yes, but only quiz shows?

The
Maths
Programme

6 You ask your mum if you can start a football club, using your back garden as your home ground. Does she say
(a) And what about the greenhouse windows?
(b) Only if you appoint me manager
(c) Yes, of course you can?

How to score:

3 a: One point

b: Another point

c: Lucky you – have you ever seen *Emmerdale*? It's a lot less interesting than being asleep in bed.

4 a: One point

b: Another point

c: Your mum thinks you're a vampire.

5 a: Minus twelve points

b: No point at all, really

c: Your mum thinks your illness has gone to your brain.

6 a: Minus ten points (and minus ten windows)

b: Half a point. At least if she's the manager she won't be able to be the ref

c: You obviously haven't got a back garden.

Score: Over three – see your teacher about taking extra Maths. Under three – join the club. You have got a mum who is *unreasonable*.

2 Training Your Mum to Stop Being Nosey

When I came to look in my postbag on this subject, I found these:

Well, what else do you expect to find in a *post* bag? Oh, all right! There were lots of letters too, every one of which had been opened and read. By my Mum, of course. Here is one of them:

Dear Aunt Aggie,

I need to turn my bedroom into a Go-Kart Repair Workshop, so that me and my mates can get our kart ready for the championships next month, but my mum is very nosey and I'm afraid she'll see. What shall I do?

Yours sincerely
Hamon Dill

I fed this letter into the MUMBO JUMBO and it replied:

And I said, "Of course it's not! It's a pseudonym I use when I'm writing my Agony Aunt column."

"Yes."

So I did.

Dear Hamon Dill,
Here's what you should do to train your mum to stop being nosey – use a red herring. You can get these at the fishmonger's for about £1·50 a pound.
Yours,
Aunt Aggie

So that was that one solved! Then I looked at the next letter in the postbag. It read:

67

Dear Hamor D'ill,

Make your own red herring using the inside of a toilet roll tube and an old coat hanger. Then say to your mum, "NO! NO! Please don't look in my room!" She will naturally think you've got something to hide. She storms in – and sees the red herring. "Ooh, isn't that nice!" she says, hearing.

"I thought for one nasty moment you were trying to conceal a Go Kart Repair Workshop in here!" She won't bother being nosy for at least a week – time enough for you to set up a Go-Kart Repair Workshop in your room.

Yours,
Aunt Aggie

P.S. Alternatively you could take up Formula One Racing instead.

So I replied:

Dear Aunt Aggie,
The red herring idea was no use. My mum's a vegetarian.
Yours sincerely,
Hamor D'ill.

3 Training Your Mum to be Reasonable

There is a very popular saying amongst mums:

"Oh, for goodness' sake, (insert name here)! Be reasonable!"

And of course, you are – all the time. Unfortunately, training *mums* to be reasonable can be very difficult indeed. It involves going Over The Top or, as it is more commonly known, "going O.T.T." Here are a couple of typical case histories.

Case History Number One

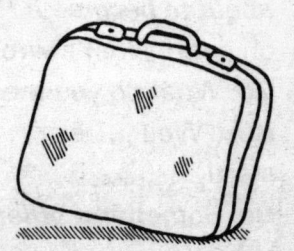

The history of this case is that it was made in 1966 by a Mr Reginald Arkwright of Northampton, and after an utterly uneventful life, turned up as an illustration in this book in 1994.

Case History Number Two

Mo Rapping wants to go and buy the new CD
by her favourite group, Got This. Her mum,
though, thinks the only singer suitable for a
ten-year-old girl to listen to is Cliff Richard.
So Mo goes O.T.T. and pretends she's into
Heavy Metal . . .

MO: Mum, can I go to the Squidgy Bogies
concert?
MUM: *(Shaking with terror)* For goodness' sake,
Mo! Be reasonable! They're Heavy Mental!
MO: Heavy *Metal* – that's right, Mum. They
really blow your brains out.
MUM: *(Terrified that her darling daughter is
about to become a Heavy Metal Freak)* Oh dear,
oh dear! What's wrong with *decent* music?
MO: What do you mean, "decent music"?
MUM: Well . . . er . . . not Heavy Metal, for a
start!
MO: Something *quieter*?
MUM: Yes . . .

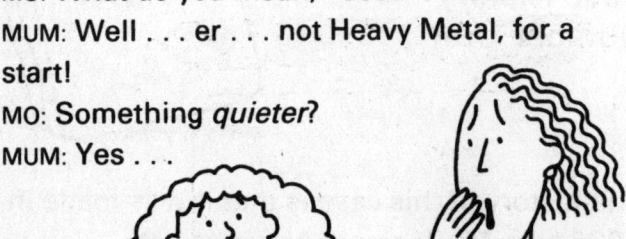

MO: Like Got This, do you mean?
MUM: (*sighs*) Look, if I let you get the Got This
CD, will you promise never ever to mention
going to see the Squidgy Bogies again?
MO: Of course, Mum.

See? Easy, isn't it?

4 Training Your Mum not to Embarrass You in Public

It's as natural (and as unpleasant) as goat's
yoghurt for your mum to embarrass you in
public.

When I asked the MUMBO JUMBO why
this should be so, it said:

MUMS
EMBARRASSING THEIR
SONS AND
DAUGHTERS IN
PUBLIC? IT'S ALL PART
OF THEIR MAKE-UP

But I shouldn't advise you to go hunting through your mum's make-up bag to find it. Because what with her Gamma-Ray Eye and Game Boy Brain, she's bound to catch you. If you're a girl this could be very awkward, and if you're a boy it could be awkward, embarrassing, totally humiliating and an utter disaster.

I'll thank you to buy your own lipstick.

The most common way for people to avoid being embarrassed by their mums in public is to *hide*.

Hiding your face

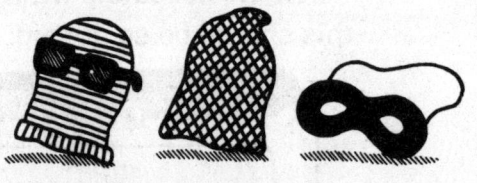

Ever wondered why bank robbers wear stocking masks? It's nothing to do with them not wanting to be seen by the security cameras, it's simply that they got fed up with their mums coming up to them in the banks they were robbing and saying things like:

"Ronnie! Get back home immediately and finish your breakfast. I've made bread-and-butter soldiers for you, specially."

Just hiding . . .

Try walking six paces behind your mum, when you're out with her. Then when she says to Mrs Noggin from five doors down: "Doesn't he take after his Aunt Vera?" you can duck behind the nearest tramp and Mrs Noggin will assume your mum is referring to a passing Rottweiler.

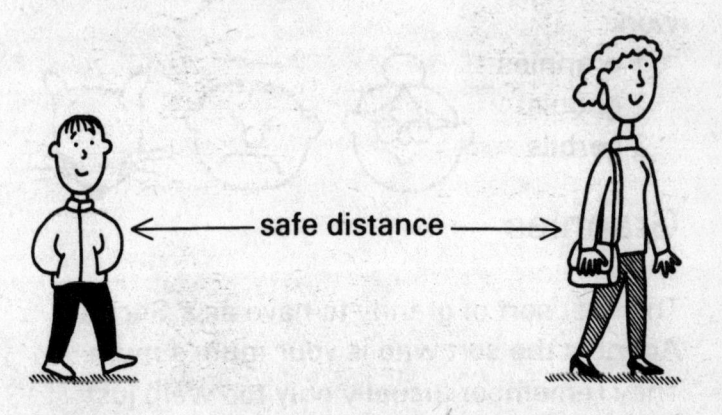

←————— safe distance —————→

However, hiding won't do anything to *cure* the problem. You really must try to *train* your mum to stop embarrassing you in public, and the only way to do this is to use *a Secret Agent* . . .

How To Handle Your Mum: Stage Seven

Using a Secret Agent

The Secret Agents you use to help you handle your mum are so-called because you keep it a secret from them that they are working for you.

There are three types of Secret Agent who are worth seeking out to help you with your work:

1 grannies
2 ghouls
3 gerbils

Grannies

The best sort of granny to have as a Secret Agent is the sort who is your mum's mum. They remember (usually only too well) just what your mum was like when she was your age.*

---

* Yes, incredible though it may seem, your mum was once a fun-loving, sensitive, totally reasonable young person like yourself!

This, as we will see later, can be very useful indeed.

You may already know of the exploits of the most famous Granny Secret Agent of them all. If you do, it can mean only one thing – you've read this book before . . .

Granny Bond 0070
Licensed to knit

Granny Bond sat in her armchair watching snooker on the telly. There was a knock at the door. In walked her granddaughter, Brooke Bond.

"Oh, Granny Bond, you've got to help me to handle my Mum!"

"Let's just call her M, shall we?" said Granny Bond. "Is she being embarrassing in public again?"

"You bet!" said Brooke.

"What's she done this time?"

"It's not what she's *done*, it's what she *wears!* Fluorescent purple and orange leggings, an old baggy sweater and beads in her hair."

"Ah! Your mum thinks she's being *cool*," explained Granny Bond.

"Cool! I should think she's freezing!" said Brooke.

"Ssshhh!" said Granny Bond, "Here comes your mum now!"

In came Brooke's mum, dressed in her fluorescent purple and orange leggings, baggy sweater and beads.

"Georgina!" said Granny Bond. "You are *not* going out looking like that!"

"But, Mum!" said Brooke's mum.

"Go upstairs and change," said Granny Bond. "You've got as much taste as a second-hand herbal tea bag!"

"That phrase sounds familiar," said Brooke.

"It should do," replied Granny Bond. "It's on page 49 of this very book!"

And thanks to Secret Agent Granny Bond, Brooke's mum never ever embarrassed her in public again by wearing her purple and orange leggings, her old sweater and beads.

Ghouls

Boy ghoul

The best kind of ghouls to use as Secret Agents are those who blow gum in old ladies' faces, swear, spit, spray Darren 4 Karen on lampposts, pass wind during school assembly and generally behave very badly indeed. There is probably at least one in your class.

Girl ghoul

Now, you may think "I'd rather suffer years of torture at the hands of my Mum, than have to talk to the likes of Lenny Lickspittle or Felicity Foulmouth," but the beauty of using a ghoul as a Secret Agent is that you don't have to talk to them at all!

The way it works is like this: your mum absolutely hates this sort of ghoul. When she mentions such people her voice takes on a tone that makes Lord Snooty sound like somebody out of *EastEnders*.

"You don't sit next to *Lenny Lickspittle* in class, surely?"

"Come away from the front window! That *Felicity Foulmouth* is passing the house."

Your mum is absolutely terrified that you will end up the next Lenny Lickspittle or Felicity Foulmouth! So here's an example of how to use a ghoul as a Secret Agent:

(Scene: Your local department store. Your mum is buying you a new coat. Her eyes light upon a dreadful anorak thing that looks as if it was last worn by Postman Pat's granny. But there's no doubt about it – your mum thinks it's just the thing for a girl like you.)

MUM: It certainly looks as if it will *last*.
(You have visions of this anorak still not being worn out by the time you leave school. Meanwhile, you have your eyes on a rather natty zip-up jacket. Time to use your Secret Agent.)

YOU: Oh, Mum! You wouldn't make me wear *that* anorak?

MUM: And why not? I suppose it isn't "cool", is that it?

YOU: No, it's definitely not "cool", as you put it.

MUM: Huh!

YOU: And the reason it's not "cool" is that it's just the sort of coat Felicity Foulmouth would wear!

MUM: *(horrified)* Is it?

YOU: Definitely!

MUM: Oh, dear!

YOU: I don't want to go around looking like Felicity Foulmouth, do I?

MUM: *(with feeling)* Er, no . . . You most certainly do not.

(Steer your mum in the direction of the natty zip-up jacket.)

Gerbils

All schools have a pet gerbil. These harmless little creatures sit around all day without much to do, so you might as well employ them as Secret Agents. They can be used in a similar way to ghouls.

Your mum probably doesn't hate the school gerbil in the same way as she hates Felicity Foulmouth and Lenny Lickspittle, but she's terrified of having the poor little thing in the house. She's afraid that it will escape, or even expire while it's under your roof. If that happened, of course, she would die of shame because the neighbours would all avoid her in the street and the RSPCA would set up an undercover round-the-clock watch on your house. So here's an example of how to use the school gerbil as a Secret Agent in the battle to handle your mum:

(Scene: *the kitchen. The problem: Your best mate Steve has invited you to go with him and stay at his cousin's for a weekend. His cousin lives a few miles from Alton Towers!*)

MUM: *(showing typical superhu-mum powers)* No, you can't go away for the weekend.

YOU: But, Mum! Steve's invited me. Wouldn't it be rude to say no?

MUM: It's the Community Association car boot sale on Sunday. I was relying on you to give me a hand.

(Yee-oww!!! This is even more serious than you thought! You'd forgotten about the dreaded Community Association car boot sale. Time to call in your Secret Agent.)

YOU: *(sigh)* Oh, well. I suppose Old Soggy*
will be pleased.
MUM: Why should Mrs Sponge** be pleased?
YOU: It means we'll be able to have the class
gerbil for the weekend after all.
MUM: *(White with fear)* What? Eh? Er, no . . .
Yes, of course you can go with Steve to his
cousin's for the weekend!
*(Time to go upstairs and start packing your
rucksack.)*

---

* *Your class teacher's nickname*
** *Your class teacher's real name.*

How To Handle Your Mum: Stage Eight

The Mum-handling Test (Key Stage 2)

Test your knowledge of mums and how to handle them in this specially designed quiz from the MUMBO JUMBO computer program.

1 Which of the following are superhu-mum powers?
☐ a Runny Nose
☐ b Radar Ear
▨ c Pain In the Neck
☐ d Gamma-Ray Eye
☐ e False Teeth
☐ f Laser Tongue
☐ g Knobbly Knees
☐ h Athlete's Leg
☐ i Game Boy Brain

2 Which of the following will help you in
   training your mum?
   ☐ a A packet of dog biscuits
   ☐ b A flock of sheep
   ☐ c A Secret Agent

3 Who would be likely to cause you more
   embarrassment if you found yourself with
   them in the local shopping precinct?
   ☐ a Jeremy Beadle
   ☐ b Your mum
   ☐ c Donald Duck

4 Your mum tells you your room is a mess
   and starts fuming. Do you
   ☐ a Ring the fire brigade?
   ☐ b Buy a mirror?
   ☐ c Tidy it up?

85

5 Which of the following is a rare type of
mum?
   ☐ a David Bellamummy
   ☐ b A Thingamummy
   ☐ c A jar of orange jam

6 What do computers believe is the source
of mums' superhu-mum powers?
   ☐ a Inter-galactic energising electrons
       from the planet Glurg
   ☐ b A handbag
   ☐ c Food

7 Why did the chicken cross the road?
   ☐ a To get to the other side
   ☐ b Because it was egged on
   ☐ c To avoid being embarrassed by its
       mum in public

8 Which of the following things should you *never* say to your mum?
☐ a "What did you do in the war?"
▨ b "Is that one of Grannie's dresses you're wearing?"
☐ c "Your home-made burgers are almost as good as McDonald's."

9 How old is your mum likely to wish you were?
☐ a Old enough to know better
☐ b Old enough to buy a car
▨ c Two and a half

10 What is the name for an occasion when your mum and your friends' mums all get together for a chat?
☐ a A coffee morning
☐ b A hen party
▨ c Nightmare on Elm Street

ELM ST.

87

Answers

1 1 point each for numbers b; d; f; h; i. Half a point for e (False teeth). This is a Superhu-*gum* power.

2 1 point for c. 1 point for b (providing your mum is Little, her first name is Bo and your surname is Peep).

3 1 point for b. If you put down a, You've Been Framed.

4 2 points for b and 999 for the fire brigade.

5 2 points for c and a 1000 whatsitsnames for thingamummy.

6 2 points for c. If you put b, then I'd like to know just what you were doing looking in your mum's handbag.

7 1 point for c. Nothing whatsoever for b – it's one of the very worst jokes I have ever heard.

8 None of them! Take away a hundred points for each thing you thought you could say to your mum.

9 Deduct 50 points for b. Score 1 point for a (every mum says this at least once a day). Score 2 points for c. All mums like to think they're a lot younger than they are, which they would be if you were still two and a half!

10 They might *call* it a or b, but of course it's c. Score 2 for c.

Your Score

Minus 1050 or more? You'll find the Samaritans' number in the phone book.

Between minus 1050 and 10? OK, you know the theory, now go out and practise it!

Between 10 and 19½? Glad I'm not your mum! More than 19½? You can't count.

How To Handle Your Mum: Stage Nine

Compiling your own Mum-handling Data Bank

Keeping a personal data bank about your mum-handling is vital, but you must make sure to keep it in a place that's safe from your mum's Gamma-Ray Eye. (Like a reinforced steel box buried in two-foot-thick concrete.)

PERSONAL DATA BANK

CONFIDENTIAL

NAME: _Alastair_

DATA ON YOUR MUM

File 1:

Basic Statistical Data

How many jobs has she got? .....1.....
(Going out to work counts as one job, looking
after you and any brothers and sisters you
may have counts as four jobs)
Height .....5.7.....
Width .....
Weight .....8 stone 5.....
(Vital information for dealing with her
Athlete's Leg powers)
Age (How old she actually *is*) .....38.....
(See opposite)

Bartering/Bribery/Buttering Up Data

*How old she would like you to
think she is*.......*32*.......

*Other soft points, i.e. What she likes to be
complimented on* (Her brains/cooking/
looks/driving/incredible wit/collection of
Abba records [see below])

O

....

Favourite group ....*simply red*....
(You can impress your mum by saying how
good they are, or by naming some of their hit
singles – if they ever had any)

Favourite TV programme ....*Ant and Dec*....
(So that you know what is positively the very
worst time to try and handle her, i.e. while
it's on)

O

Favourite brand of chocolates ....*cadbres*....

There are certain days in the calendar when
buttering up can work especially well. These
days are:

Mother's Day (date varies) ....*17th March*....

Your mum's birthday (date)....*Jan 12*....

CONFIDENTIAL

Your birthday (date) .... 23-2-93 ....

Phobias (i.e. spiders/snakes/your sweaty
trainers)..

Her attitude to you

*What she calls you when she's cross with
you* ...... naughty ....

What she calls you when she's really *cross
with you* ..... grounded ....

*The person in your class she most wishes
you were more like* ..... myself ....

*The person in your class she's most glad you
aren't like*..... Tom ....
(See p.77: Using Ghouls as Secret Agents)

*What she wants you to do when you leave
school*..... football ....

CONFIDENTIAL

92

NAME:_____

DATA ON YOUR MUM'S SUPERHU-MUM POWERS

File 2:

Radar Ear

O The longest distance from which your mum can pick up the noise of anything you shouldn't be saying or doing (in kilometres) .... 2 kilometeres ....

Gamma-Ray Eye

The thickest substance your mum can see you through:

Quite thick substance (bucket of sludge) — YES/~~NO~~

Really thick substance (bucket of stodgy custard*) — ~~YES~~/NO

O Really really thick substance (two buckets of stodgy custard*) — ~~YES~~/NO

Unbelievably thick substance (your big brother's/sister's head) — ~~YES~~/NO

Available from your school cook.

Laser Tongue

The usual word your mum calls you when she's cross with you, using the N Index (words beginning with N)

Nerd	YES/NO
Nincompoop	YES/NO
Nigel	YES/NO
Nitwit	YES/NO
N.E. Other?	......

Athlete's Leg

Your mum's running style when she chases you upstairs to your room. Does she:

Hop like mad	YES/NO
Run like crazy	YES/NO
Leap like a frog that's sat on a firework?	YES/NO

Game Boy Brain

Work out your mum's Game Boy Brain IQ by:
Adding her age to the number of teeth she's
got .....70..
Subtract the number of records she's got by
Cliff Richard ...66...
Multiply by the number of times a day she
says "When I was your age" ....132........................

Your mum's Game Boy Brain IQ is....Blue.....

File 3:

Secret Agents:

Name Maiy
Code name Ma   O

Name Sedastion
Code name Bcz

Name Joseph
Code name Joe

Name Tomas
Code name Tom

Name Alistair   O
Code name Ali